# WHITE**GHOST**
## THE KEN LE BRETON STORY

# WHITE**GHOST**

## THE KEN LE BRETON STORY

JON JON WHITE

TEMPUS

IN MEMORY OF NORRIE ISBISTER

A good, kind and wonderful friend sorely missed.

This book is humbly dedicated to all those riders who gave their lives, whilst participating in a sport that they loved and cherished, and also to all the forgotten survivors who suffer still, in great pain from injuries received in the pursuit of speedway greatness.

First published 2003

Tempus Publishing Limited
The Mill, Brimscombe Port,
Stroud, Gloucestershire, GL5 2QG

British Library Cataloguing in Publication Data.
A catalogue record for this book is available from the British Library.

ISBN 0 7524 2873 X

Typesetting and origination by Tempus Publishing Limited
Printed in Great Britain by Midway Colour Print, Wiltshire

# CONTENTS

# TESTIMONY

As Ken's only surviving sibling, I feel honoured to have been invited to add a personal testimony to his memory. In our childhood years, Ken was the typical brother to his siblings except in one respect. He was always protective of me. 'Nobody dare touch his little sister.' So, as for me, I have only fond memories of growing up with a loving brother.

Our dad, Frank, was Ken's most devoted admirer and mentor, from his very first practice session to trying to give some comfort in cradling his son's injured head in that ambulance ride to the hospital, from where he was never to regain consciousness. I cannot imagine a more devastated father.

Ken loved and respected his mother. During his final unconscious breaths, as we stood around that bedside, his last and only word was 'Mum'. I wondered if in some way he sensed her presence.

Over the years, much has been recorded of Ken's many deeds and accomplishments, as our photo albums and yellowed press cuttings bear witness. They have been lived out, and passed on. But it is the 'spirit' of the man that lives on. In this biography, Jon Jon captures the true 'spirit' of my dear brother Ken.

Marie Mitchell (Ken's sister)

# APPRECIATION

I would like to extend my heartfelt deep appreciation to Ken's sister Mrs Marie Mitchell (née Le Breton), her husband Sam Mitchell and their lovely family for their belief and enthusiasm. They are charming and wonderful people whose kindness knows no bounds. They told me so much about Ken's early family life and provided many of the rare photographs. This book is for them.

# AFFIRMATION

*They simply would not listen to me. I said to them, there are people not yet born who will come to marvel at what this young man tried to do. Words borne out of sadness have stood the test of time. Ken Le Breton, the White Ghost, is dead, but his spirit and soul live on…*

Ron Johnson, the former New Cross captain, speaking on the occasion of the first anniversary of Ken's death.

# COMMEMORATION

Ken was essentially a quiet man, gentle, kind, often very shy and retiring. The brash loudness and aggression of his image was his alter ego. He loved his work beyond anything else in his life. What a wonderful joy for a man to have been able to work at what he loved best, with the people he knew and cared for around him, to achieve the heights of success in his profession and to be remembered with love and affection by so many. He dreamed a dream and the dream became a reality.

Kathleen Le Breton (Ken's sister)

# ACKNOWLEDGEMENTS

There can be no easy beginning or ending to this list of thank-yous. I am indebted to the encouragement, support and co-operation of Ken's former friends, and to the many fans who never actually saw him race, but still fell under his spell. They shared everything they had – their memories and their boxes of old treasures. They read my notes and transcripts and then the draft chapters, and lost almost as much sleep over them as I did. They thanked me for having helped them to ensure a pride of place for a very remarkable man, who meant something special to each of them. I am particularly grateful to Willie Wilson, Ken's friend and teammate.

I will be forever indebted to the strong and admirable people who loved Ken: his family. Theirs is a dimension always present, but too seldom explored in the telling of this story. The glory of this book is theirs; the mistakes and omissions are mine.

Thanks are also offered to the National Archives of Australia; Colin Garbutt of The Defence Service Records, Australian Army Soldier Career Management Agency; Mr D.F. Gibson of the Australian Government; Carlton and Rank Organization; Wessex Films; *Speedway News*; *Speedway Post*; *Speedway Star*; *Speedway Mail*; *Speedway Gazette*; *Speedway World*; *Broadsider*; *Vintage Speedway Magazine*; *Newcastle Chronicle/Journal*; *Glasgow Herald*; *Glasgow Evening Times*; *Evening Citizen*; *Scottish Daily Record*; *Daily Mail*; BBC Scotland; Karl Magee of the Mitchell Library in Glasgow; the librarian and staff of the Newcastle Civic Library. Special appreciation must also go to Gordon Dobie, Hugh Vass, Brian Darby, Jim Shepherd, Rob Andrews, John Jarvis, Robert Bamford, John Chaplin, Mike Hunter and Barry Wallace.

It has been virtually impossible to ascertain all the names of the photographers. We duly acknowledge Frank Le Breton, Allan Gerrard, Norrie Isbister and Molly McPhee. To all those others who helped in this project, no matter how small the contribution, you all displayed nothing but kindness itself.

# FOREWORDS

This book powerfully brings to mind the numbing shock which I felt when I heard that Ken Le Breton had been killed in a racing accident in Australia. The news swept rapidly across the country and I imagine that almost all those who were involved in speedway at that time shared my feelings. Ken was the personification of all that we wished to be and his death seemed almost unbelievable; indeed, for a time rumour was rife that it was a hoax. This could be considered odd, given that those of us involved in speedway were used to losing friends and comrades, but Le Breton was someone special – had he lived, he would surely have been World Champion in another year or two.

During my association with him (a mere couple of years at Glasgow's Ashfield track), he had been more than an employee and comrade – he was also my friend. Due to the passage of time, I think it has been forgotten, and perhaps not even fully comprehended, that he was also a man.

Faced with this legend of the 'White Ghost', Jon Jon set himself a task of deciding and explaining what he was really like. Many other writers in their own various fields have sought similar objectives before, but there can be few who have faced a more difficult problem. A life that was over in only twenty-six years is not an easy prospect to write about; it is even harder for a life concentrated on speedway, for it is a kind of specialised way of living, which even now is not thought of as being an admirable way to make a living. A life that became a legend in its own time tends to portray the image, not the identity. At this point I must say that I take some of the blame in encouraging Jon – but when he did speak of his intention of writing this book, I had grave doubts as to how he would fare and whether the book would ever actually see the light of day.

The initial reading of what he has written so far has vindicated my belief in him, and he has succeeded admirably. Jon gathered up the pieces and dissected the legend, separating the myths and reconstructing the man. In doing so, he shows us that Le Breton, far from being first amongst equals, gifted with virtues and skills, was in fact a rather ordinary person, and not even endowed with particularly good health. Le Breton the man and his achievements now

appear all the more remarkable and all the more heroic than the legend itself.
Jon has set Ken Le Breton in an abiding place, to which legend and rumour
might have otherwise, ultimately, denied him.

Norrie Isbister
Glasgow, 1989

I put Ken in the category of not only being a great rider, but also one of the
world's leading speedway personalities. He was a real patriot, had a rapport
with the fans that few other riders have ever had, and they duly responded to
him and saw him in a different light. They never somehow seemed to com-
pare him to other riders. There was always a kind of special, honourable place
for Ken. Other great riders came before him, but when Ken arrived on the
scene, he mapped out a place for himself and as a result became well
respected. It was a thrill for me to have been in the same team, and to have
ridden alongside him. Even speedway riders have their favourite riders and
Ken was definitely mine.

Willie Wilson
(Ashfield/Belle Vue)

I don't really feel I'm qualified to write about Ken as he was one of the very
few great post-war riders I did not have the pleasure of seeing in action. But,
you certainly could say he was the embodiment of the unique showmanship
gifted to only a very great few in any walk of life and that he is a ghost that
will forever haunt wherever and whenever men ride racing motorcycles.

Dave Lanning
(Speedway journalist and broadcaster)

# INTRODUCTION

There can be no question that Ken Le Breton was a star, universally loved as a human being. He was also thoughtful, intelligent, studied and articulate, and able to write and verbalise his thoughts on many subjects besides speedway, his first love. The strength and happiness of his marriage to his wife, Joan, represented something priceless to them both; she, in her own quiet manner, helped Ken sustain his love of speedway. Ken did not give many interviews, but his answers read like an oral history of his times. He was always diplomatic, but there didn't seem to be a question he would not answer, and there is no reason to believe that everything he did say and write was not 100 per cent truthful. Of course, Ken does not answer all the questions we would have wished to have answered.

In his tragically short life, Ken brought immense pleasure and joy and many long-lasting memories to the thousands of supporters who appreciated what he brought to speedway. He exhibited a fiercely competitive spirit that was both excitable and unforgettable. He was far, far superior to most of the other riders of his day. He was a first-class technician and noted for his highly developed style of riding. A fair and decent rider, he never resorted to foul or unfair tactics. He would always gracefully acknowledge the endeavours of his fellow competitors, especially when he was defeated. He generated a genuine warmth in all who came into contact with him – fans, promoters, the media, fellow riders and track staff.

Ken Le Breton's impact upon the public and his resulting fame is unique. His talent and gift for communication made him extremely popular wherever he went, but out on the track he was different, although still as charismatic as ever. Ken's warm and generous personality ensured him great respect and admiration, as was his concern and consideration for all men and women regardless of their position in life. His intelligence and wit were legendary. In the unreal world of speedway, it takes a strong man to pursue a career and still remain a genuine, decent person. Ken made sure that speedway never took over his real self.

For those who were touched by his presence either on or off the track, the experience was dramatic. Captivated by his unique force of racing speedway, they became lifelong believers. His vulnerability and honesty, his daring, and the sheer beauty of his kind of stylish riding, cut through to their hearts, and it remains there still. The enormity of his image and the magic of his persona for those who were fortunate to have seen him during those few short years, riding all sorts of tracks in all kinds of conditions and various settings, leave them with a frustrating experience in trying to describe what they had witnessed. He was endowed with the greatest gift a man can have — talent.

# One

# BATTLING THE ODDS

Francis James Le Breton was born on 15 August 1924 in Kogarah, Sydney, New South Wales. At home, he was Frank junior to the family; his childhood friends called him Jim. In the Forces his buddies named him Ken, but the world knew him as 'The White Ghost'. It was around this time that dirt-track racing, or speedway as it soon came to be known, also came into being.

As a child, he was highly spirited and mischievous. At school, he tried his hand at everything, but excelled at nothing. It was only with the onset of war that signs of a special calibre begin to emerge, and even then only gradually. During this period, Ken's first priority and achievement was to survive. Thereafter, his combat experience became an asset, and his resolution and strength of mind now had something definite to aim at: the hard, harsh, cruel world of high-speed motorcycle racing, at which he was to excel, and ultimately give his life to. Surprisingly, very little was known and understood about Ken Le Breton as an individual. The problem lies in deciding what he was really like. To reconstruct a lost life from brief glimpses and faint echoes has been a long and difficult process, even more so when its adulthood has scarcely been reached.

In the society of those heady days of the 'boom years' of speedway, relationships were often intense, measured in snatches of time for what he had achieved rather than what he was. Fifty years on, it is hardly surprising that a lot of what people remember about Le Breton was that he was a 'good bloke'. Only those that knew Le Breton well can take us closer. Even then, the insights only go so far. Le Breton's wife produced a brief memoir recently, but her portrait reveals surprisingly little about the man her husband was.

The recollections of the promoters and staff at the various tracks where Ken Le Breton rode are inclined to be of a vivid, bustling nature; everyone remembers a decent, fair-minded person, who was not above cracking a joke or two. Ken was essentially a very determined man, which seldom takes us any further into his psyche. This was not their fault, as a rule Le Breton did not mix closely with those whose duties did not expose them to the same dangers that he and his compatriots faced. His relationships with his fellow riders were far more intimate, and to Le Breton rather more special than he was able to achieve with outsiders. The private opinions of his mentors are even harder to ascertain, for many have long since passed away. Perhaps, as Johnnie Hoskins himself once remarked,

*That Le Breton was as great a rider as speedway ever bred, his natural aptitude for inspiration and leadership was unquestionable, his outstanding skill was only matched by his bravery. Extremely gifted.*

Hoskins freely admitted that any conversations he had with Le Breton were always brief, and to the point. Others, outside Le Breton's circle, claim they were impressed with his gutsy performances, but that he was nothing special, and was always thought of as another stunt of Hoskins. What was unusual about Le Breton was that he lived long enough for his staying power and experience to combine into an endeavour of utter single-minded profession-alism. If objectivity is elusive from these quarters, those within his circle are equally hard to come by with some degree of accuracy. Willie Wilson, a for-mer teammate, who rode both for Ashfield and Belle Vue, remembers that:

*Ken had this kind of aggressive stance, legs slightly apart, straight upright, hands folded across his chest. His face seemed to be kind of pugnacious, the chin just pushed forward a fraction, teeth clamped, but his eyes always gave him away.*

What drew a person's attention to him were his eyes. They were a greyish blue, full of sparkle, but with a hint of action or mischief, behind which laid a more complex, complicated, contradictory and very vulnerable person. Le Breton is well remembered by all those he ever came into contact with for his verve and charm. Again, there are those who say he was opinionated and self-centred. However, his employers and those in authority found him to be disarmingly modest. In fact, in most of his time in speedway, he always 'had' to impress peo-ple time and time again, a tendency to which his colleagues reacted in differ-ent ways, but seldom with indifference. As a front-runner, he was both feared and admired, often impulsive. Sometimes, although not as often as some have declared, he would go off the deep end and might be rather annoyed, but these moments were few and far between. Le Breton attracted far more companions than he did close friends. This was a special relationship that was reserved for those who could accept him on his terms, and he had a great respect and tol-erance for all of those who shared his love of speedway.

Some of the contradictions regarding Le Breton can be resolved by his strongest traits, an ingenuousness which enabled him to confront authority and people, his close relationships, and whatever tasks were at hand, as well as a directness and astute versatility. This simplicity meant that his friendships were all approached wholeheartedly, and his opinions were all frank – this type of openness could enchant and antagonise in equal measure. It should be borne in mind, however, that these traits depended upon his given circumstances at any given moment – the surroundings, the company kept, previous lessons learnt. Behaviour and responses can and do change a man, especially in his early life, and more so in time of war, when Le Breton was forced to mature very quickly.

Le Breton's unrelenting enthusiasm for speedway racing was always a source of comment – he seemed to have no sense of fear, and many perceived that he was perhaps a glory hunter. It is an undisputed fact, however, that towards the end of the 1950 racing season, those around him began to detect symptoms of apparent restlessness and irritability. Amongst his speedway associates, he remained outwardly steadfast; it surely goes without saying that he would have confessed his real feelings to his wife, Joan. However, the question is not whether Le Breton actually knew about this anxiety, but just how he managed to keep this fear in check. When asked if he was frightened of dying, he replied by saying: 'No, not really. I have friends waiting for me up there – when the time comes, I will be more than pleased to see them all again.'

Until that day arrived, he lived and worked hard, pouring all his energy into his chosen career. He had faced death before, it was nothing new to him and he simply took each day (and race) as it came. This may explain why he was at ease with himself. Having survived terrible jungle warfare, he had managed to prove himself wrong, so he deliberately embraced speedway with its constant threat of death as one might crossing a busy street. He had seen Death's face before, and it had ignored him. It was not ready for him, but when it was, it made no mistake. His death was unnecessary, a self-fulfilling prophecy.

Le Breton was a born leader. To those who worked with him, there was no question about that. He knew exactly what he wanted and he also knew how to get it. It wasn't a matter of being stubborn; it was just that Le Breton knew what he was doing. His attitude was that if he couldn't race a speedway machine, then he had no business owning one. There was nothing phoney about his self-confidence. He was a strong man, and like all strong men, he wanted to have things his way. Usually he got it; if he didn't, then he wanted to know the reason why. Strong men take a delight in tackling roadblocks, but when they can't meet them face to face, then no amount of inner fortitude will help much.

The world of speedway is a mixture of all things to different people. The build-up to a race and the atmosphere at the track can be intoxicating. The one overriding factor is that the public always enjoy themselves, whilst at the same time appreciating the efforts of those who are doing what they probably all dreamed of doing themselves. In the arena there is an air of expectancy and anticipation, of settling down to an entertaining evening full of high excitement.

Behind the scenes it would be no less exciting. However, here, it was a different kind of world, and it could be a fascinating place to be in. It is a scene of organised ritual, unpacking and assembling, preparing machines and equipment, not forgetting the heated arguments that can often occur. Nerves also play their part, and everyone seems to have their own way of dealing with them — it comes with the territory, and playing the part of a performer. Some crack endless jokes, some are quiet, some chain-smoke; all the riders would be aware of the inherent risks of their chosen sport, and have established some kind of inner peace within themselves.

Ken Le Breton arrived in speedway with a ragged reputation, no better, no worse than any other novice eager to make his mark. He was often blindingly fast, but along with his pace, there was a cautious edginess, which would vary between the extremes of reckless abandon and a supreme reluctance to turn the power on. He walked away from his early accidents relatively unscathed, and pursued a policy of putting into practice his mechanical and riding talents that was on occasion simply ferocious to behold.

His career was extremely brief, consisting of barely four years. He started when he had just turned twenty-one, after his demobilisation from the army in late 1945. His best year was undoubtedly 1949, when he achieved a great deal, and the future held the promise of better things to come. It was tantalising. One never knew what he might be capable of, for he had already reached the World Final that year. In the months that followed he was sometimes struggling due to occasionally sloppy, error-strewn riding. More often than not, however, he was world class — untouchable — and turned in fantastic performances when they were least expected. He was an expert at precision racing and was a joy to behold on the track, having the silkiest, smoothest of touches. The off-days never seemed to faze Le Breton — he took each race as it came. He genuinely loved the sport — to be involved was all that he asked. It is all the more remarkable that he succeeded, having deliberately chosen the hardest way possible.

If he had decided to become a writer, no doubt Ken would have excelled at that too. We do know he was commissioned to write a series of articles for a weekly or monthly column in various newspapers and magazines. The majority were written under his own name, and it is believed he also acted as a ghostwriter for other riders. However, very few of his articles were actually published, and we are left with only a few fragmentary pages to pick at. The impression, which unfortunately cannot be really substantiated, was that he may have objected to the articles being rewritten or tampered with, and that he withdrew his consent. As it was, his forte was speedway; he became a top-class rider, very much in demand, and this was where his greater ability was on show. It may well also be that the content of the articles were too controversial and serious. If the old speedway magazines of those days are read today, the majority are jocular in tone. On many an occasion, Ken was quite outspoken about this, stating that if those who reported speedway failed to take it seriously, then the public would do the same. Being a man of principle, he would not have subscribed to such levity. He always demanded 100 per cent support. A quiet and modest man, he would have been an easy target.

Even the press couldn't ignore the days when the angels appeared to have touched him, reducing his speedway rivals to pedal pushers, and endowing the scribes with broken pen-nibs. There were other times, though, far too many some might say, for a rider of Ken's calibre and talent, when no matter how hard he may have tried, his presence at a meeting went unnoticed. He would oscillate between sublime self-confidence and dithering uncertainty. His ability could be quite quixotic and unusually complex – he was perhaps too sensitive for a speedway rider. However, he was somehow able to draw inner strength from deep within himself and produce some great racing.

Ken wanted that kind of psychological support around him – he needed to be aware that everybody was pulling for him. If everything felt all right, then he was unbeatable. He was able to channel all this goodwill and spiritual energy into his own motivation and concentration. Being an honourable man, he didn't steal a race from a teammate who trusted him on the last corner of the last lap. For someone like Ken, that would not have been winning a race, for he had too much integrity and pride to even contemplate doing anything like that.

He may well have thought he could influence the powers that were in control, as to the way ahead, by showing how things ought to be organised and operated. Reading between the lines, it was more than likely that his association with Johnnie Hoskins (a man who had had many a bust-up with authority over speedway matters) meant that Le Breton was also placed in the same category and considered *persona non grata*.

In a long conversation with the 'great man' himself, one evening in the summer of 1977, Johnnie Hoskins commented:

*Ken was indeed a very determined person, and the more obstacles that were put in his way, he had this natural inclination to surmount the problem by attacking it from another direction.*

He was emphatic about one point though:

*In years to come, it will not be the powers that be, not the promoters, or even the hacks, who will be remembered for their contribution to speedway. It will be those riders who strove to present speedway, as it ought to be. These chaps needed to be listened to. And I don't mean the riders who seek to secure an influence via a brown envelope. If the riders are not listened to, then the future of speedway and its eventual outcome will be reduced to a meaningless stupid event full of nonsensical regulations, like fox-hunting, pin-bowling, where is the social standing in that? Ken said all of these things and more; he tried to get the young ones involved. Yes, I know times were different then, and life was hard for lots of folk, but he showed them the opportunity for self-motivation. I saw in him, myself, as I ought to have been. We didn't mix socially, that sort of thing, but we shared many similar thoughts. He was very intelligent and had a great capacity for seeking the truth. I guess the war did that to him. He lost some good friends, I know. It sometimes bothered him, but he seldom talked about that.*

It was clear that Johnnie Hoskins vividly remembered the impact his star rider had on those around him at the time and in the aftermath of his death.

Success, when it came, gave Ken Le Breton a distinct professional status, quite disproportionate to his age and standing. He had to work long and hard to achieve that level — to maintain it meant that he had to keep on producing results. His personal record made him one of Johnnie Hoskins's favourites, so Ken was able to further upgrade his own ideas and tactics. His relative youth may have been looked upon as an intrusion into the running of a heavily-financed business had it not been for the unique quality of Le Breton's erudition. A legendary figure was beginning to emerge out of the youthful ace and leader. He was mature far beyond his years, something upon which many of his family friends often remarked. This developmental gulf between Le Breton and his contemporaries was further enhanced by his military service. His ghost-like ability to appear and vanish without ever saying very much earned him a quiet respect, admiration and deference from his army comrades.

An old family friend, who was also a physician, describes him thus:

*Francis was a very beautiful man, almost too beautiful to be a man. He was handsome, darkened hair, slim. His features, very finely chiselled, were perfect and he had a profile that caused people to turn and stare at him. His complexion, skin texture and colouring were not surpassed by the most beautiful of women. BUT... there was absolutely nothing feminine about him in any way. His piercing stare and his unmistakeable acceptance and exercise of authority, caused contemporaries, subordinates and superiors alike to listen and to obey. He was well educated and a highly intelligent man, with an exceedingly good character, that guaranteed everything else about him. He had this direct line of thought, and was astutely analytical of all around him. He was nobody's fool. He had a good self-discipline and control without harshness, and had this under-standing of faults in others, that is rare, but he had no understanding for anything that went against that understanding.*

Ken Le Breton also had a great strength of principle, and with it went deep devotion; in a more abstract sense, this enveloped any cause, speedway or oth-erwise, which he embraced. With such devotion went great warmth and no one felt the glow of this as much as his wonderful wife, Joan. Anyone who was close to the couple knew just how devoted they were. Few people on the out-side really knew Ken. He was a naturally shy man. He was never an extrovert. To get out in front of the public was not an easy task to begin with. He knew what people expected of him – a glamour boy, dashing hero type. Such man-nerisms didn't come naturally, he had to work hard at that too, and gradually his charm slowly surfaced, to which people responded wholeheartedly. His quiet sense of humour was his foundation in life and this saw him through.

Nobody can deny that he did everything that was expected of him. His contribution to speedway was tremendous. How much greater it might have been, nobody will ever know. One can only guess. He was an outstanding teacher and instructor to those who would listen. He could teach them to race and win. He gave special attention to any new rider who followed his credo. He would take them aside, indoctrinating his methods and demands that would leave that particular rider thinking that he had done the opposite. Le Breton had a gift for tactics, being a very practical man with an outstand-ing imagination.

Le Breton often came across as thoughtful and quiet, one who seldom smiled, but photographs do show that twinkle in his eyes. He took his respon-sibilities seriously and to heart, pouring all his energy into his work. He lived his life with a quiet Christian dignity that no inferior individual could ever breach.

He was, in every respect a 'gentle' man. His inner strength, combined with his formidable riding and tactical skills, was turning him into a champion for which it seemed that all his life had been but a preparation. Somehow, Ken knew, deep within himself, that he had been blessed with talented gifts, but he also knew that he had to work hard to bring them about and to perfect them, then refine and polish them, again and again, until he had no equal. He was true to himself in that he was humble, and it is quite possible that he may have felt that he was the best rider of his day. This, of course, does not mean he was better, or not as good as any other riders from his time or earlier, it is just that a comparison is simply not feasible.

## Two

# IF DREAMS COME TRUE

The riders who changed speedway were inspired. There weren't all that many of them, but probably the most notable was Tom Farndon, who came to prominence in the early part of the heyday of speedway. He was a true legend in his own time – a time when styles, engineering and mechanical know-how brought speedway to a level of compatibility, whereby all riders had a fair and equal chance. The sport reached a point of sophistication, of total seriousness, and was strictly monitored and guided by a set of rules and regulations. Farndon was able to capitalise upon this aspect and he set about blazing a trail that was suddenly and abruptly ended when he died in 1935. Sadly, for lovers of speedway, just as they were slowly getting over this blow, the nation was plunged into a long, drawn-out war in 1939.

It would be nearly another seven years before speedway sought to re-establish itself, only this time there would be many more incursions vying for the public's attention. Speedway fell back upon its pre-war position, seeking to pick up the scattered pieces. Most of the heroes of the past were now in their mid-thirties with a few older still, desperate to recapture an interrupted career, only to find that they were not as daring as they once were, caution had now crept in. Luckily for them, the new younger generation of riders was few and far between. In Britain, National Service was compulsory, brought in during the war. It lasted until the early 1960s, and what is more, wages, unemployment and rationing were still very restrictive for any young man contemplating a career in speedway. The country was recovering, but it was taking time. Most jobs were low paid, and nearly all were apprenticeships, followed by military service.

The demand and cost of new racing engines, which were mainly hand-built, meant there was a long waiting list. Added to this was the prohibitive cost of the rest of the equipment – frames, wheels, tyres, chains, carburettors, leathers, helmets, as well as the purchase of suitable transport. The whole gambit of being an independent self-employed rider was not to be taken lightly. It was a risky occupation at best, never mind the threat of serious injury or worse. The rewards were heady, however – glamour, status, money, travel…

Any young rider with the right application could easily reach the higher ech-elons, and reap much gain. This, in turn, could set them up for life. The lure was all too powerful, and appealed to many young ex-servicemen's aspirations.

One such was Ken Le Breton, whose own career would more or less emulate that of Tom Farndon, and would cause the same lamentations. He was never the innovative genius, as some would claim, yet, apart from changing the role of a speedway rider beyond recognition, he also provided the undoubted inspira-tion for his own and succeeding generations of riders. With his charming good looks, and his great presence both on and off the track, he left a lasting visual image of what is now commonly known as the 'boom years' of speedway. It could be said with some justification that Le Breton saved speedway. He was a dedicated, hard-working rider, a non-smoker and teetotaller, as well as a kindly, spiritual man. He set an ideal and a pattern that was hard to follow, but which would be a requirement of those who sought to take up the sport. His image, riding style and personality were all shaped by the times through which he lived. It was a time for toleration, mutual respect of others, the law and author-ity, and, regardless of who a person was, where he came from, his situation, class, creed or culture, the individual was judged by his own merits.

To try and understand what made Le Breton become the man he was, it is mindful to know a little of the background of those years, the places where he was brought up, where he lived and worked, the tracks he rode, the riders he learnt from and against whom he raced. In seeking to explain that background, it is possible to determine the measure of the man, who in his own unique way helped to forge a lasting impression of that era of speedway history.

To have achieved international acclaim and status in so short a time period is all the more remarkable when Ken's origins are considered. Born and raised in a working-class suburb of Sydney, Ken could quite easily have slid into a life of dull humdrum mediocrity, enduring the monotonous round of repeti-tive sameness either in some factory, on a shop floor, in manual labour if he wasn't clever enough, or perhaps in the wide loneliness of a farming lifestyle that was the lot of many young men at that time in Australia.

Le Breton had a goal that was not to be denied – he had had a burning desire to be a speedway racer right from a very early age, and nothing was going to be allowed to stand in the way of his achieving that goal. In seeking to fulfil that ambition, he was aided by a fortunate sense of timing, for there was no better place in which to grow up than in what was surely recognised as the birthplace of speedway itself (although the sport had previously been referred to as dirt-track racing, originating in America in the early 1900s). It proved to be a combination of events that comprised of solo machines, sidecar units, midget cars (which often used motorcycle engines). It was a new sport, exciting to watch, and even more exciting to participate in. The prize money was good, which appealed to many young men with a sense of adventure and fun.

Ken's father, Frank senior, was no exception, and he became a moderately successful rider. Ken consequently grew up with speedway being a common topic of conversation, with mealtimes spent discussing the great racers of the day. There were days when the family would go out to watch the racers in action; Ken would return home to bed, to dream of one day joining this elite group.

The passion would have grown with him through the years. Ways and means would be sought to achieve his perceived target. To be able to ride a motorcycle competently is primarily to have no fear of the resulting speed, but to have faith instead — faith in the reliability of the machine and in one's ability to control it. He would have received a great deal of support and guidance from his father, and coming from a loving, stable family background provided plenty of encouragement.

Speedway fans loved Ken Le Breton because they saw something of themselves in him. He was not from a wealthy family, his background was humble and plain, and when he went with his father to solo sidecar events it was in much the same spirit as the thousands of small boys who probably went out fishing with their fathers at the weekend. Ken had worked hard at meaningless labour out of necessity, and had served his country, loyally and proudly, during the Second World War. Using his savings, gratuities and demob pay, Ken bought some 'well-used' second-hand equipment. He received no handouts; nobody, apart from his father, came along to help or to back him. His situation was one that anyone who has worked hard to earn a few pennies can identify with. Receiving no help is often a mixed blessing, for it meant that he depended upon no one but himself.

Ken Le Breton was perhaps one of the most talented and gifted of riders of the immediate post-war era, but like so many other great riders of that time (Jack Parker to name but one) he was never to become World Champion. One factor has to be taken into consideration when discussing the merits of the various riders of those bygone days — the reliability of the machinery. The JAP racing engine was the best of its generation, but it was inclined to suffer from poor valve seatings, so a rider had to be a bit of a mechanical genius in order to get the most out of an engine (and to finish a race). Ken's adopted practice and stated doctrine was to try and win races at the slowest speed possible. The majority of riders are unable to do this as excitement or bravado usually takes over. Not everybody had Ken's determined wherewithal to stick to a pre-planned method. He often said that driving a machine flat-out in every race only increased the chances of an engine failure.

In the late 1940s, the standard of engineering and servicing of racing engines was practically non-existent, which meant a rider was obliged to do most of the workshop maintenance himself, although some clubs did have a resident mechanic *in situ*. Ken looked after his own machines, spending endless hours working out calculations, magneto settings and timings, piston rings and strokes, tyre pressures, long frames and short frames, correct balancing of wheels, angles of handlebars, the list grew with each meeting, as he sought fractions of improvements here and there. It was only when he became more successful that he was able to employ a mechanic to assist him.

No matter what kind of mechanical power is involved, each and every detail has to be taken into consideration. Ken believed that having excess power in reserve enabled him to compensate against someone winding it up going round on the outside. Ensuring that the rear wheel wasn't spinning coming out of a corner meant that the machine could be driven faster along the straight. A reliable engine, and using one's head, meant he could compensate. So it was not always about speed. Different tracks required different variables and settings. There was never any need to tamper with the fuel provided the chemical compounds were correctly measured and blended, ensuring that the oil was of the right texture, and that the flows were kept spotlessly clean and dirt free.

So what was the Le Breton magic that created this hero worship? It could be summarised as a unique blend of race-winning ability, showmanship, courage and an affinity with the public. That alone would have been sufficient, but there was more besides. Many riders often seemed remote and aloof; this was not Le Breton's style, however – he would spend many hours chatting and signing autographs, long after a meeting was over, no matter how tired he may have been. Quite often, he could be found welcoming fans at a turnstile before a race or even wandering in amongst the crowd, shaking hands and thanking people. He took the sport to them, personally.

His racing appeal was down to total commitment, that he had perhaps had more courage than was believed possible. Le Breton could take a race by the throat and never let go. He gave it 200 per cent all the time. His races somehow seemed to be that little bit more exciting than they may have been for any of his more successful opponents. He could pass them on the outside with a skill that was simply breathtaking to watch, or could hold the white line as if he was welded to it. He could win races with wheel nuts loose, flat tyres and even broken handlebars – he always seemed to be at odds with something or somebody.

Astride a machine he was fantastic; in the pits, he was not always the easiest man to get on with. Few people ever reach the top by being totally relaxed, easy going and amenable. He was a perfectionist who could take offence easily and he was never slow to protest, arguing his point with force. He was tough on those around him, but he was tougher on himself. Demanding, dogged, determined, aggressive, sharp and quick, he could step up a grade and leave other higher division riders standing still on their own tracks with relative ease.

Speedway racing was, and always will be, spellbinding to watch. It is packed with tension when you have evenly matched riders and machines racing on a well-prepared surface. Le Breton tried to ensure that this was always the case whenever and wherever he rode. However, he was also prepared to be cunning if required. He was quite prepared to annoy everyone by foregoing his 'White Ghost' image at tracks where promoters had treated him with a lack of respect. Dressed in the same way as the other riders, the promoters would get the rider as billed but not the image!

As his success grew, there were those who sought to cash in on him, and what he was able to bring to speedway. Many promoters were 'get rich quick types' who were seeking to take advantage of the conditions in the years immediately after the war. There have been comments that Ken could not handle the pressure of coping with the media spotlight and the attention of appearing in public. This is utter nonsense. He was well used to crowds and public arenas, right from his early days travelling around with his father. After his time in the Forces, Ken was also well-versed in conducting himself in public.

For the speedway public at large, Le Breton breathed new life into the sport. Whereas before it had been mostly pre-war riders seeking to regain their former status, there was now a new air of optimism. The original old-timers had been brought up on the atmosphere of circus-like entertainment, with riders dressed as clowns, machines that belched out sheets of smoke and yards of flame, female riders, children on mini machines, handicap races, 12 or 20-lap races, last-man-standing races, pantomime — it went from the ridiculous to the sublime. There were the usual money-making sharks, cigar-chewing, hard-headed businessmen who were out to make a killing — backhanders and double-dealing were rife.

Slowly the poison had been got rid of. It had been every man and promoter for himself, but now order and regulation were rigidly enforced. The antidote was the new breed of arrivals, such as Huxley, Frogley and Farndon, who led the way and were followed by the likes of Le Breton, Warren, Hunt and Forrest a dozen or so years later. They were not prepared to tolerate shenanigans and demanded the sport be given the respect it rightly deserved. Riders thereafter became the focal point and were willing to give their all — a constant reminder that speedway was now a serious business.

Of all the great riders of the past, none was more serious in his intent and endeavour than Ken Le Breton, and ever since he has continued to intrigue and fascinate speedway fans throughout the world. Although Ken never referred himself as 'The White Ghost', some unknown commentator or publicist placed that burden on him as a form of callous ridicule, which duly backfired. For the rest of his career, Ken tried to leave it aside as much as possible – it was simply a means to an end, designed solely for the purpose of getting rides wherever and whenever he could, until he could get established.

Leaping ahead in time, the added attraction of riding for one of the most unforgettable speedway teams in the long history of the sport, the much lamented Ashfield Giants, only reinforced his status. Part of his involvement with the club was, through Hoskins's entrepreneurial ideas, that the rest of the team were to be similarly decked out in a selection of colours – red, blue, black, brown, grey, silver, yellow and black – with every rider made to contribute in some fashion. The rainbow-hued Ashfield Giants provided a brand of speedway that was both colourful and exciting to watch. They boosted attendances wherever they went. The opposition invariably raised their own level of commitment in order to compete against Le Breton and his cohorts, obviously inspired by their leader's magnificent image. Nothing quite like this had ever been seen before; to this day, little has ever come close to matching it.

For those who never saw them, photographs can't really convey the magic and splendour of what it must have been like to witness and experience. Except for Le Breton's premeditated inception of his image, it is worth repeating again: that he deliberately set out with this in mind, knowing full well that the bulk of the photography for media purposes of those days was predominantly black and white, especially as most meetings in Australia and in Britain were held in the evenings under floodlights. The majority of riders, apart from Le Breton, wore either black leathers or ex-military dull dark brown, and the machines were made from unpolished steel components. After one race, every rider was covered in a layer of a thick, wet mixture of crushed cinders or greasy shale. If one was a casual observer to speedway, it was extremely difficult to tell one rider from another, except perhaps by helmet cover or a number on the back of the race jacket.

Ken's father was also a part-time professional photographer, working at weddings and other celebrations. He was also occasionally employed by the Sydney Show Ground Complex to cover sporting events. Ken and his father had discussed this approach in great detail. Novices and juniors have always had great difficulty in obtaining rides. They would have to practise on the beach or a piece of waste ground, and wait in endless queues at some training session to get a few laps in. Sooner or later, the novice has to try his luck in public. It can take nearly three hours to give approximately sixteen riders just four or five rides each per meeting. Often there are perhaps forty or fifty novices seeking rides at any given meeting. So, the chances of getting just *one* ride at any meeting were always going to be difficult. His appearances were thus all the more memorable because of this impact. It cannot be disputed that he added to the gate. His performances on the track were as dramatic as his image. Le Breton's aura and sheer magnetism reached out to people, and it was all done with great panache and style.

It is all about presentation, the sight and sound, the image, the riders, the fans. The mighty Ashfield Giants were all that and more. A smooth well-oiled and drilled machine, soldiers on parade, the whole organisation worked long and hard to achieve the correct results and image. Much of this smooth professionalism came about from the fervour and belief created by Norrie Isbister and Johnnie Hoskins. Consequently the supporters responded in a similar manner, coming through the turnstiles in ever-increasing numbers and making Tuesday nights at Saracen Park definitely the place to be.

On the surface, the life of a speedway rider may have appeared to be very glamorous. However, the reality of life on the road was very different. A trip down south meant perhaps five meetings inside a week, providing very little chance to wash and sleep properly, far less get a decent meal. There were constant travel problems, either by road or rail: stiff, sweat-stained leathers that stank to the high heavens, covered in layers of mud, hands grimy with dirt and oil, fingernails split, thumping headaches, the body sore from head to foot. Day clothes clung like rags, having been slept in. Glamorous? Far from it.

Speedway folk are only in it for what they can get out of it — this is mostly enjoyment and self-satisfaction. The last thing on their mind is the public's perception and image of them. All they are concerned about is their riding and their machines; they would rather spend their valuable time concentrating on that, rather than worry about their so-called easy lifestyle. Promoters promote and riders race is the oft-repeated cry, but both sides quite often miss the point.

The old-fashioned image of 'wall of death' riders from the Australian outback and wild cowboys from the USA who simply powered their way around a race track, and 'mad road-racers', still persisted from those very early days. Full of playboys and wing-walkers, speedway had that kind of pull. The circus image — the gladiators in the arena, the ever-present threat of death or serious injury — was a huge attraction in the beginning, and some promoters, to a lesser degree, believe it is still there today.

Those original Ashfield Giants from Glasgow were really something else! They showed how speedway ought to be. Glaswegians are a no-nonsense kind of people who have pre-set notions of their likes and dislikes. They vote with their feet at the drop of a hat, if they think they are being conned or ripped off. They can, and do, appreciate sincerity and intent. The Ashfield promotion gave the public that and more. The racing was invariably close and top notch, the second halves were 'do or die' cut and thrust affairs with many of the leading top-flight riders of the day being invited to challenge for the big money prizes on offer. Hardly a week went by without Le Breton defending his prowess in special match races against the next new challenger. There were also many special International Matches and Cup Matches against Division One teams; the Ashfield supporters were used to the best, and they also got to see some of the world's best riders too. Norrie Isbister said at the time:

*What we are trying to do is to set a fashion in speedway. People here in Glasgow and the surrounding districts, work long and hard trying to live decent and honest, upright lives. They want something that reflects that. They also want something a little bit different in the way of entertainment, that they can call their own.*

A fashion in speedway? Certainly, Johnnie Hoskins was one of a kind, always one step ahead of everybody else. Quite often, he may have been one step to the side rather than leading the way, but the 'fashion' he instigated was both thrilling and magnificent, and with the benefit of hindsight, his Ashfield Giants were arguably the most entertaining team of all time.

They were a hand-picked mixture, entertainers and characters one and all, comprising of experienced veterans that Hoskins had known previously, others he had heard about, and others still who had been recommended. Never one to stand still, racing or otherwise, Johnnie actually loved the business through and through. Le Breton came under that spell and caught that free-flowing spirit. Where once it had been much of a muchness, a dull plain sameness, a magic wand was waved. Surprisingly, it worked.

Ken le Breton – the White Ghost, Keith Gurtner – little Boy Blue, Merv Harding – the Red Devil and Willie Wilson – the Wasp. Eric Liddell was usually in grey/silver, Bob Lovell in old-fashioned, dirty, scruffy leathers, Larry Lazarus in his blue and white hoops, and finally Alec Grant, whose preferred option was any colour as long as it was black. Last but not least, there was the one and only Bruce Semmens, of whom it was said that everyone had their own description! When Bruce arrived at Ashfield, his reputation followed him. He was, at first, treated with a cautious respect; few spoke to him, except Ken, who embraced and welcomed him wholeheartedly in his own charming way, so much so that Semmens was completely taken aback at this encounter. He also fell totally under the Le Breton spell and, unbeknown to Ken, took it upon himself to be Ken's protector and ward off the sharks!

After Ken's untimely death, life for the fabulous Giants took a downward turn; some would remain, but others drifted away – without Ken's presence, the side lost the cohesive spirit which bound it together.

# Three

# A LULLABY OF HOME

Ken would have made a good Scot. As a nation, they are noted for being a cautious race, never rushing in until it is thought through first and everything digested. Risk-takers they are not, being both very determined and stubborn, for they never give up. These are also good attributes for a speedway rider, in that he can direct his resolutions into the right areas and make it work.

Le Breton's forebears could well have been exiled Scots forced to flee their native homeland as a result of their loyalty to the Jacobite cause, and may have first settled in Brittany (Ken's mother suggested perhaps Guernsey) before finally emigrating to Australia in the early 1900s.

So, here the Le Bretons settled anew and built themselves a life in search of freedom and opportunities, not only for themselves but for the generations to follow. Frank Le Breton and his wife Mary were God-fearing people who worked hard to sustain themselves and their five children, three sons and two daughters. Of the three sons, only Ken progressed into manhood. Leonard, his younger brother died before he was quite four years old, and his baby brother, Louis, passed away shortly after birth. His sister, Marie, is now the only member of the family left, as her elder sister, Kathleen, passed away recently. Marie, a charming and delightful person, is happily married to Sam, an ex-speedway rider himself, and a very nice, kind and undemanding gentleman. They now live in peaceful retirement in a lovely part of Australia.

Life was hard for the Le Breton family, as the huge worldwide depression hit Australia hard. These were not good economic times to be raising a family, but Frank senior was luckier than most, for he had a steady, reliable job as a locomotive engineer/fireman. It was still a precarious life for his wife and children, however, they were poor but happy. Their lives were more or less bound by the working-class suburb of Lakemba, which lies to the west of Sydney. A quiet residential area with broad streets well laid out, most of the properties were detached timber structures with scrub gardens. Ken's home was located in Wangee Road close to the local Belmore Primary School, which he attended until he was about twelve years old, before going on to the adjacent high school.

As soon as the children were old enough, they were encouraged to look for work, berry-picking, shopping, newspaper rounds, collecting and delivering laundry washing, dog-walking etc. The family's constricting poverty gradually began to ease. Frank senior soon began to entertain the hope that his children might rise in the world. Nobody would have to remind them that someday they would have to go out on their own and earn a living. They were a happy and contented family, full of interest for each other. Mother Mary was a renowned cook, well-liked for her warm, generous hospitality and disposition. As for Ken's sisters, Kathleen acquired her mother's looks and charm, as did Marie with her wit and grace. Ken himself was indulged early in life by his mother, due no doubt to the tragic loss of his younger brothers.

However, of the stresses and strains of family relationships, Ken had little to say, other than he was well into his teens before he had learnt to replace anxiety and distress with a calmer and stoic attitude. His mother was mild-mannered and consistently kind. She had infinite patience and always seemed intent on keeping the peace, rather than fighting back. Yet she appeared to have an inner strength that carried her through unpleasant and trying situations. Ken often thought that he took after his mother, although his inner strength did not manifest itself until much later.

From his earliest years, Ken was fascinated with imaginary games, either with school friends or on his own. He was a small and rather delicate child and although he frequently got involved in playground rough and tumbles, he was careful enough to avoid situations that would lead to serious fistfights. This may have led him to become much more physically strong; he remembered well the personal and communal fear engendered by local bullies, who took pleasure in beating up any youngster found on his own.

Ken was reserved and shy as a youngster. However, he apparently told his schoolteacher that during playtime girls were always following him – not bad for a boy of seven or eight. It is clear that he had begun to show the independence that was to become his trademark even then.

He had enormous respect and affection for his parents and his sisters. They were role models for him, his conduct, propriety and even morality. It was a close-knit family that required much of him, but he often thought that perhaps they expected a little too much. Still, Ken was astute and careful enough of the family's feelings and always tried to give the right impression of love, honour and devotion to them. Outsiders had to be very careful not to intrude upon these sensitivities.

The family were not overtly religious in the true sense of the word, but being Baptists they accepted the Biblical teachings and drew great inner strength from having strong beliefs. For Ken, this meant that there was much more to life than materialism, so his intellectual ambitions were typical of those years when people believed that if you were going to do something, you ought to try to learn something and know something. Some learn from going to college, others from reading, and some from conversations. When people did ask questions, Ken would say, they *knew*, if you knew what they had been taught, you didn't ask for a sight of diplomas or certificates, they just knew!

Going on to high school separated him from his close childhood friends, and the new friendships formed were mainly superficial. So throughout his teens, he was pretty much a lone wolf, going to the cinema on his own or accompanying his father to the various racing circuits, perhaps reading or messing around with motorcycles, and going for long walks with the dogs. He attained a kind of suave, Ronald Colman-type sophistication, although he was still extremely shy and an introvert. On the sports field, he was a poor performer — his abilities were often erratic and below average. Enforced participation meant that his efforts regularly drew good-humoured, though still hurtful, derision from his classmates, which made him retreat still further. In spite of that, he was very well behaved, highly organised and had no real bad habits. He maintained this image very deliberately, for his parents had taught him the importance of commanding respect.

It was a dignified stature and a hard one for any young man to discipline himself to. He was seldom, if ever, to stray from that belief. Of course, like any normal youngster, he was full of high spirits, and got into the usual high jinks — nothing out of the ordinary, and this was a phase that passed quickly. This stateliness suited his nature; with anyone else this can cause much stress and mental tension if it is merely put on as an act. Not so as regards Ken, his sense of fair play and decency was there for all to see. His family had struggled hard and lived by and preached the simple but honest meanings of life. They taught their children that a healthy mind creates a healthy body, and that cleanliness is next to godliness.

His academic and sporting achievements were never ever going to take him onto a higher level; domestic circumstances and finance precluded that avenue. In any case, he felt restricted by the current prevailing scholastic doctrine. He knew he had an inquiring mind that required an outlet and quickly realised he would gain more by his own efforts. His father helped him to build an outdoor gym so that he could do his own physical training, combining this with long-distance runs, callisthenics and weightlifting. Ken knew he was lucky. Everyone is entitled to their fair share of luck, but that was usually found to be in the hands of the gods, and they are careful to whom they dispense that luck. To earn it, you must first have the chance, at least, of finding it. There was no influence, no fortune. Fate had put him into a position in which he could distinguish himself. He had that spark of originality by which a man might create something completely unique by some instinctive alchemy of personality, ability and opportunity.

Ken didn't have to look very hard to find something he would shine at. Ken's father was a solo and sidecar racer of some note and there was often good prize money to be had. Unfortunately there wasn't enough to make a full-time living out of it, but enough winnings came his way to stay in the game. There is an old adage which says like father, like son and Ken inherited his father's love of motorcycles at an early age.

Ken was indeed lucky, as Frank senior spent a small fortune on motorcycles; every spare penny was saved, not to be wasted on tobacco or drink and other so-called pleasures. He could also tune engines and build his own frames with equal ease. Frank was a kind, homely, genial, cheerful and generous man, and was greatly respected about the neighbourhood. He had a wonderful way about him, much of which rubbed off on Ken. Consequently, much of Ken's young life was spent in and around the world of motorcycling, which he grew to love in its entirety. It may have been a somewhat unusual childhood, but it left him unaffected, for it was normal for him.

Sadly, the longed-for breakthrough was never to happen, for his father and he achieved only moderate amounts of success. In spite of this, however, young Ken was enthralled by it all, tagging along, holding spanners, filling the tank, changing the oil, watching, listening and learning all the while. What he couldn't find out from his father, he would have surely found out from the other riders. He lived in the local libraries, reading books about mechanics and engineering, especially those concerning racing engines.

Travelling around the circuits with his father gave Ken an insight, denied to other aspirants, and, more importantly, time in which to assess the dangers and pitfalls of the sport. He also became aware of the hero worship that went with the status of being a hotshot racer, along with the adulation, the flow of adrenaline, the big cash prizes, the trophies, the cheering of the crowds, and of doing something that most other folk could only dream of doing.

Of course, it was just a simple father and son relationship, a bond that linked them. Trust and love – there can be nothing finer. Frank senior taught his son all that he knew about racing engines, stripping them down, fine tuning and rebuilding them, how to build his own frames to suit the different kinds of tracks, all and everything relating to dirt-track racing. The one thing he could not teach was experience – Ken would need to acquire that himself.

However, as they discussed Ken's future, dark clouds were looming on the horizon. Ken was about to finish school. Britain was now at war, fighting desperately, and common sense told them that Australia would become more heavily involved with the passage of time. If it did drag on, Ken would be obliged to serve his country. It was clear that the first thing to go would be the simple pleasures in life, such as motorcycle racing. Perhaps it would be more beneficial to get a well-paid job and save his money in war bonds instead.

Sister Kathleen remembered that this debate caused a bit of a family squabble, as Ken's mother was upset that most of the young men were joining up. As she saw it, Ken's immediate future looked far more dangerous than racing motorcycles, and yet here were father and son planning and scheming, calm as you like, for after the war! It was a worrying time for all families who had sons. All anyone could do was to hope and pray and get on with their lives. There was an air of euphoria that it would soon be over if Australia, along with all the other Commonwealth countries, sent troops. Ken and his father managed to calm her fears for a while, but deep down, according to Kathleen, she felt a huge dark shadow come over the family and she was never was quite able to dismiss it. Regretfully, Ken's parents were soon to divorce, something that was very difficult for the whole family to come to terms with.

The whole country slowly began to gear up for a faraway war. Frank senior spent longer and longer hours at work, leaving the family to draw in and pull closer together whilst everyone watched and waited. A crossroads in young Ken's life was now fast approaching. He was smart and clever, and before long there would be many opportunities for work. He was advised to find a job with good wages and to invest as much as possible so that there would be a nest egg waiting for him when the war was over. Besides, they had reasoned, there would be no racing until after the war.

Ken had his own ideas about his future, but he was rather phlegmatic about it. He was a patriot who loved his country and the way of life that it gave him and his family. However, Ken wanted to take up speedway seriously, and planning for such a career required capital. His father had proved that it was possible to operate successfully as a privateer, but only as a sideline hobby. To be serious about speedway and to earn a living from it meant he would have to go where the sport was both highly organised and well paid.

This required him having to leave home to try his luck in Britain. It would cost a lot of capital just to get there, find a team, secure a contract, survive at least a year, and still have enough to get home if it all went sour. In the meantime, all he could do was to dream. With family finances being what they were, higher education was a little beyond his grasp, especially with a military call-up before too long. He had little choice, but it did seem as if the way was being shown, he would try his luck down that pathway, he would find the highest-paid job he could and save as much as possible in the intervening time left to him. Much as he would have loved to find employment in a garage, he required something that provided good money and the opportunity to earn more.

Ken secured a well-paid job with a large manufacturer of optical equipment as a lens grinder and setter. This was a very highly skilled occupation, which required much technical expertise and concentration. He would have to wait until he was sixteen before he could begin work there, so he hunted around for a job to fill the intervening period when he left school.

Good wages were to be found locally in the nearby tobacco factory, which produced all sorts of tobacco products and by-products for medicinal use. It was foul, stinking, smelly work. Tobacco factories were dangerous places; the poisonous nicotine fumes claimed as many victims as the devotees of the weed. Small wonder Ken was a non-smoker! The labour was menial, and the intelligence required also minimal. He obtained employment, and before long quickly rose to become a charge hand/foreman, working all manner of hours and shifts, and helping to provide the resources to pursue speedway in the interim.

By the time Ken turned seventeen, the national press, radio, and cinema newsreels were proclaiming that the most noble thing any young man could do was to serve King and Country. The generation that Ken belonged to was raised on patriotism, and unquestioning reverence for men-at-arms. Pearl Harbor had changed everything for everyone. The Japanese were now bombing the Australian mainland, and everywhere Australian troops were facing reverses and disasters, from North Africa to Malaya. The life Ken had known was now gone – nothing would ever be the same again or so it seemed at the time.

The only bright spot at this juncture was that he fell hopelessly in love with a small, strikingly beautiful girl called Joan Minnett. They had been friends since childhood, but they now saw each other in a different light. He remembered her teasing him from those days, and concluded that he had indeed loved her, but from afar, and Joan had responded likewise.

As Kathleen cast her mind back, she recollected that Ken would often recall their very early childhood memories.

*Especially the family reunions at Christmas. These were splendid affairs, dinner was often late, and it would take all day for friends and family relatives to arrive, bringing extras for the table, so that meal preparations were constantly being interrupted. Long trestle tables groaned under the weight of food – apart from the usual traditional fare, there was a barbecue on the go non-stop and long after the meal was finished there would still be someone at the table. People came and went, children played games, and the usual card games started. There was always a fiddle, or a guitar and accordion, so we played and sang. There'd be barbershop harmonies, womenfolk with delightful voices, and always a beautiful rich Irish tenor, who could move you to tears — and a huge bowl of punch that somehow never seemed to empty, and friends and relatives could be seen adding tipples. And, of course, everybody was called upon to do a turn — sing, or do magic tricks, recitations, charades, pantomime — and Ken, he had a delightful sense of humour with good one-liner jokes. Mum and Dad were usually cajoled into doing a kind of Irish jig, matching each other's steps. Dad was a big hearty man who chuckled a lot when he danced, and Mum, well, she would surprise us all, she could dance perfectly still with just her feet and ankles moving at speed. Her cheeks glow a bright pink, and her hair would curl around her forehead. When they finished, they both would collapse on a settee and giggle like a pair of naughty children as everybody cheered and clapped.*

*We had some wonderful times then — even though we didn't have much, they did the best they could for us. Those were hard days for most folk — plenty of leisure but no money, but we somehow seemed to have a lot more fun. The good times were good. People read a lot, we did crosswords together, or we all listened to the radio. The music was really good, lots of plays, give-away shows, comedy programmes. There was always something to do; tennis was very popular, visiting the beach, picnics. Then there were local amateur nights in the local community hall; whist drives, and it was always some-one's birthday. Movies were cheap. Ping-pong was also a big craze, bingo, too. Country fairs, farmers buying and selling, prizes for everything, rodeos, stalls with bric-a-brac, home-made cakes, patterned quilts, yes, a great day out for one and all.*

*Like most families, our parents would spend a few evenings trying to assemble our family tree. They didn't speak a great deal about their own childhood, so I guess it must have been a very trying time for them. I know we lost some relatives in the First World War, and the families were scattered afterwards, some distant cousins remarried and moved away. People had to go to where they could find the work, I suppose. Dad always said we came from good Scottish stock — born of Kings, Lords of the Isles, he would say. He thought we belonged to the MacDonald clan; I do know he was a mem-ber of our local Scots society. As a family, we felt Scottish at times, and most of our fam-ily friends are also Celtic people — we seem to have got on better with them. Nearly everybody can trace their roots back to Ireland or Scotland. Maybe that's why Ken liked Scotland — I know he loved the place and the people.*

They say it is between the ages of eighteen and twenty-one that a youth becomes a man. Ken was to become an adult in the midst of a terrible war fought in the jungles of New Guinea. Any sense of normality and assimilation was slowly shattered during those desperate years, as friends and comrades would appear and vanish overnight.

So, like many other young Australians, he joined the army. He had joined up after asking permission from his parents, which says much for his character and his upbringing – much more than a whole page of other people's opinions would ever reveal about him. Most of his friends had already gone, Ken was alone and he felt it. There was that sturdy hardiness of his forebears in his blood, and this would stand him in good stead now. He soon found comrades in the Forces, most were either first or second generation Australians and, like their ancestors, the closer to danger they came, the calmer they became. 'It meant fighting, and that scared me stiff!' Ken told a friend.

His only real worry was his eventual posting. The Japanese were all around Australia, and it had become so bad that the Government was obliged to bring back a whole Division from North Africa to reinforce the defences and to expand the new intakes. He remembered his embarkation leave with a fond longing, back home amongst his family and friends, having his pet dogs constantly running at his heels, a pleasant return to normality which he would have been glad to prolong. He was obliged to register for Military Service on his eighteenth birthday, and passed his medical having been classified A.1. He enlisted on 9 September 1942 as NX173031 Gunner Le Breton at the Belmore Recruiting Depot for basic training, which lasted ten weeks. On 28 November 1942 he was posted to 1st Aus Light Art A/A Training Regt at George Heights, outside Sydney; upon completion of this training he was seconded to 1st Aus Heavy A/A Regiment at Greta (further up the coast) which was scheduled for deployment in New Guinea. However, the Heavy Artillery Units were found to be unsuitable for operations due to conditions. So he became RTU to the 1st Aus Light A/A Regt proper.

He was given three weeks embarkation leave before being posted to the 9th Bn 2/3rd Art. A/A Regt, which was then transferred to Townsville in Northern Queensland for a period of acclimatisation and operational training prior to deployment in New Guinea. The regiment landed in Port Moresby early in November 1943 (the height of the monsoon season) and commenced operations as part of the Australian 5th Division on the Huon Peninsula, which was preparing to relieve the 9th Division. The various units within the command provided defence for airfields, supply depots, transport as well as initiating combat experience. Le Breton served in a wide variety of duties until early 1944. During this time period, the torrential rain never let up, huge prolonged thunderstorms turned the countryside into swamps and seas of mud, which caused widespread flooding. With daytime temperatures soaring into the 100's, the troops fought a constant battle with dehydration and heat exhaustion whilst under constant enemy fire.

During the first week of March 1944, Ken's unit was at a forward airstrip unloading ammunition supplies from DC3s, and helping to load wounded for the return flight, when, late in the afternoon, they sustained a heavy air-raid.

According to army records, much damage was done and many casualties were taken, one of whom was Ken. Apparently he got caught in the blast and was knocked unconscious and flung many yards into the brush. He was discovered the next morning, still unconscious and suffering from some sort of fever due to exposure to the elements — it was still raining heavily. An insect, probably a scorpion, had also stung him, for his right arm was swollen and had turned purple. His body was covered in running sores from insect bites.

Ken was taken to a casualty aid station, where he received first aid treatment. From there he was evacuated to 2/7th General Military Hospital at Port Moresby, where he was diagnosed with dengue fever and BFPN (Battle Fatigue Psycho Neurotic). On top of this, he also had swamp fever, malaria, heat exhaustion, concussion, minor shrapnel wounds and a temperature of 105.

Most of these injuries were treatable in time, except for the malaria. A mosquito 'bite' is actually a blood-sucking action which leaves a parasite (plasmodium) which affects the red blood cells within the body; this parasite reproduces itself at recurring intervals. There are many variants of malaria, and at least four of them are nearly always fatal — one of the worst kinds is called plasmodium falciparium, which attacks the brain and the kidneys and results in severe mental and physical illnesses. Further mosquito bites only increase the fever — the symptoms of such attacks are first a chill, followed by shivering, prolonged sweating, violent headaches, aches and pains throughout the body and delirium. This can last on and off from forty-eight to seventy-two hours. Then, miraculously, the patient suddenly recovers, depending upon the kind of malaria he has been subjected to. Quinine has long been the most useful of drugs in the long-term treatment, but malarial attacks and fever will occur without warning at regular intervals for many months or years later. The problem was that Ken had a particularly virulent falciparium strain, prevalent in New Guinea, which was resistant to anti-malarial drugs available at that time.

After a month in hospital at Port Moresby, Ken was shipped back to Brisbane and the military hospital there. He was discharged from further frontline military duty by the end of April 1944, and remained as an outpatient for the next eighteen months while he slowly recovered; as for the battle fatigue, the only treatment prescribed was rest and solitude. Ken was finally demobbed in November 1945, having lost almost three stone in weight, being nearly blind, extremely depressed and suffering from panic attacks.

It was not surprising to discover that he hated talking about his experiences, for in truth, as he himself said, he was barely conscious most of the time, and he couldn't remember even if he'd wanted to. So Ken did what he always did – he kept his wartime experience to himself, burying it deep at the back of his mind. His military record and demobilisation papers outline only the barest of details, but the same also applies to many other servicemen.

The way in which Ken suffered during the war is highly relevant to the state of his health at the time of his death. Today we are acquainted with the notion of shell shock, battle fatigue, and post-traumatic stress disorder, and much more is known about how to treat this form of illness. However, it was not until the Falklands War that the British Government took any notice of it; the Americans and the Australians woke up to the reality of the illness in the Vietnam War, but, back in 1945, stress-related illnesses simply didn't exist.

# Four

# NEVER TRAVEL A STRAIGHT ROAD

Ken had about him an aura of almost ethereal calm, seldom raising his voice, whatever the circumstance. It is said that people from the Western or Channel Isles have an air of placid aloofness, a kind of arrogance native to them alone. When asked, Ken replied: 'Not so, 'tis but a shyness.'

The faintly mocking smile on his face would convince any unbeliever. He was positive that the right rewards would come his way in the fullness of time, but only when he was ready. His appearance off the track may have led people to think otherwise – clean-shaven, smart, well-dressed, he looked more like a businessman than a dirt-track racer. At his chosen profession, however, he really put in the effort. Climbing off his machine at the end of a race would reveal him red in the face, gasping in huge gulps of air, with rivers of sweat pouring off his forehead and his hair dishevelled. He clearly gave it everything he had.

For all the softness in his voice, his steely ambition was never in doubt. Apart from the simple joy of racing around any kind of track, his motivation seemed to dwell upon the thought of one day being World Champion.

*If I thought there was some reason that I was unable to win it, then I would quit this minute and walk away from this madness. I have no desire to spend my life in it just for the sake of it.*

There are stories that circulate of top riders who, when they are having a bad night, pull over and blame machine problems. When this was said of Ken, he replied with some sharpness: 'You cannot imagine how a rider feels about something like that!'

There was a degree of reluctance in some quarters to acknowledge his class. He seemed to have no weaknesses, did well on most tracks, regardless of the conditions, and won more than anyone else. For some reason, those people who never knew the man believed they wouldn't have liked him even if they had known him. When asked for his comments, Ken thought for a long moment, and then said in his typical quiet Aussie manner:

*There is a lot of hypocrisy and deceit within speedway. It is not always about winning but how you race. This is the passion. There have been some champions who were not all that good. Also many riders, who seldom won races, but were simply great and should have. How about those who lost by the width of a tyre? Better still, the riders who never give up and come in last. These fellas come tops with me. Life is a game; if it were otherwise it would be very boring. So winning all the time is boring. The idea is to set standards so that everybody has a chance of winning. You must understand, winning is only part of it, I am happy to be in speedway. You cannot imagine the thrill when you finally have it all come together. I love racing. So I guess, I will keep going as long as I still feel this way.*

Ken spoke with good humour and dignity, which left the questioner totally embarrassed at asking such stupid and idiotic questions. He then emphasised his point:

*I will tell you this though, if you care to listen. There is a line of thought, that if you go to the Gate once too often, they just might open. No matter what form of high speed is involved, say surfing, or how about high-board diving? It is simply a throw of the dice – you have as much chance of winning as losing, each time you go out there, no more than last week, say, and no less. I have already seen the dark side. We all have fears to live with, deep inside of us. When you realise, on a daily basis, that somebody is trying their best to kill you, you reach an acceptance with yourself. At the moment, all is going well with me. True, there are times when I feel that none of this is worth the hassle. I have achieved a certain amount of fame, and this has given me a chance to view all aspects of human nature. Many people have been very nice and have said complimentary things. That is generous of them. I have also seen sheer wanton violence and greed. On the whole, most folk are decent and that hides the lower level types. So I have learnt to appreciate my privacy – that is why I love going home, there I am a nobody.*

This was a comfortable philosophy for any rider to have. Fame and fortune do go hand in hand, but it can be a double-edged sword. Earning one's living as a sportsman entitles the customer and the media to have their say. Everyone gets their share of flak from time to time – cynical criticism and snide remarks – and this can encourage others to join in.

To give an insight, there was an occasion when Ken showed his dispassionate and calculating side. Ashfield were the away team. The home team required a 4-2 score in the last heat to win. At the end of the first lap they had precisely that. Ken was lying in second place behind the home rider, who only had to hold his place for the next three laps. However, an in-field photographer striving to get closer to the action stumbled and fell unconscious across the track.

There he lay as the riders passed on the second lap. For some unknown reason, the officials saw fit to ignore the situation, whereupon Ken took it upon himself to halt the race and slowed down the third and fourth place riders. Needless to say, the home-team rider who was leading went through the roof, hurling foul abuse at Ken, who stood calmly beside his machine, looking on without emotion. In the re-run, Ken allowed the home-team rider to resume his first place, while he shepherded his teammate from the third spot, keeping the other home rider at bay to ensure a division of the points.

Thereafter, Ken became more voluble as regards safety matters both on and off the track. He always claimed that his motives were solely altruistic. It has to be said there were others who developed a strong antipathy towards Ken and as such their feelings never changed. There were whispering campaigns, the kind that sharp news hounds pick up. Being a realist, he was well aware of his worth at any given moment. It was a matter of pride with him – right from the very beginning he simply refused to pay to race. The wheeling and dealing that went on left him inwardly angry. Ken looked upon speedway as a livelihood and a business – it had to pay him. Straight as a die, the frankest of the frank, he could put up with anything but dishonesty. Life may change, but people don't. He found himself apart from the mainstream of 'that' society; however, he had to live within the auspices of a life in the fast lane.

Once, every now and then, there comes along a man whose talent and personality somehow seems to mingle and lift him onto another plateau in the public's affection. This quality cannot be defined, let alone manufactured. Ken would fight as hard for fourth place as for first, and would never accept defeat. It wasn't so much his pace that entranced the fans, as much as the style that came with it. Often the machine was like a bucking bronco, forcing him to race harder than he cared to. There is no greater sight in speedway than a rider controlling a machine beyond its limits. Few can do it; even fewer have the courage to try.

Ken raced with obvious passion, joy and enthusiasm – this was evident to all those who were watching. His sublime skill and masterful control, coupled with a fierceness that was simply quite frightening to behold, were a rare combination that was irresistible to fans of speedway.

His standing as a 'rider's rider' was unquestionable. However, his inability to gain true recognition which was his by right was denied and long overdue. There was another signpost coming but it seemed so far ahead and so, for the moment, he couldn't find the time to concentrate upon it. He could ride an impeccable line, deadly in pursuit of others, inducing them to make mistakes, whilst making none himself. His style reflected his character and personality – intelligent, calculated, ferocious in making his opponent's weaknesses work for him, utterly ruthless yet fair. He would give racing ground if anyone sought to take him on.

None other than Jack Parker, who had many a fine race or two with Le Breton, said this of him: 'That youngster gives me the shivers.'

That was indeed Ken's motive – he really could put the wind up other riders. Often remote, some thought Ken was arrogant, but more often than not he was simply deeply in thought. Like all top racing motorcyclists or drivers, he lived for himself. He tried to surround himself with the best, although the best was a sleeping bag in the back of his van, perhaps an uncomfortable night's sleep on a train, or on somebody's sofa. Ken could rough it when the need arose. What many people apparently did not like about him was the fact that he didn't try to hide his attitudes or feelings. He would display a pitiless professionalism or hostility towards his competitors, merely inwardly laughing at them. There is no sweetness in defeat, and some could never reconcile themselves to that indignity, especially coming from someone like Ken.

Jealousy, that was all it was, pure and simple. There will always be people like that. However, in spite of that Le Breton managed to capture the hearts of speedway fans in two continents, and nowhere more so than in Scotland. He seemed to fit everyone's idea of what a dashing daredevil speedway rider ought to be. His sense of humour, often droll and quick-witted, sat well with his slight Australian accent, and he would often have people smiling. He had a kind of bonhomie that people found attractive, but he was under no illusion as regards reaching out towards people in general. He knew exactly how good he was and he didn't try to hide that fact.

Success had been a long time in coming – he had suffered the ridicule along with the humiliation in silence, and he had continued to smile through it all. It was a case of waiting for his talent to reap the rewards he deserved. He had started late in speedway, but he did have one advantage – the fear factor had long since vanished. Like all the true greats, he detested anything that wasn't genuine – the phonies who only came around in the good times, the rich youngsters who bought their way in, the know-alls who knew nothing, the gold-diggers who made money out of the sport at the expense of the riders, the cheats, gamblers and con men, the rip-off merchants – but the people who really annoyed him were those who refused to take the sport seriously.

He excelled on any type of surface, be it greasy, treacherous, slick, rock-hard, cinder or shale, clay or dirt – it made no difference, for he had a delicacy and a feel for racing that was truly unbelievable. He would tend to arrive as early as possible at whatever track, unwind by going for a walk and take in the sights, then have a light snack, and perhaps take a nap for an hour or two. Then he would slowly and methodically begin his preparations, unloading his equipment, getting set up mentally and physically; he was renowned for not being hurried in any way at all by anyone.

Afterwards, he would walk the track in reverse, looking for the riding lines, uneven spots and the parts that had been repaired, and measuring the widths on corners, particularly the drive points going into the corners. This was always done with great care and observation. He would then walk the line that he planned to ride, again with meticulous scrutiny, checking the depths of the surface at various locations. The safety fence was also closely inspected, especially the parts with solid fencing, for it bothered him that there was no set standard – they could be either chain link or wooden (the railway sleeper type), and there was also quite a noticeable variation in heights. Some tracks had sheet steel plates, and a few even had corrugated iron roofing sheets simply nailed to wooden support posts. Ken also had a habit of carrying a claw hammer plus a blunt chisel on these manoeuvres, knocking off blunt nail heads and hammering flat sharp edges. He would often seek out the track staff, cajoling and badgering them for assistance, using his guile and charm to good effect.

The referees and track officials were always the last people to turn up at a track, most of whom were little better than well-meaning amateurs, who got paid a pittance for their endeavours. Ken would often demand that they should be, at least, seen checking safety measures and medical facilities instead of taking them for granted. Of course, the gung-ho types would snigger behind his back at these antics. Some might be safety conscious, but many said that Le Breton protested too much and was rocking the boat unnecessarily. It would be many years before the stricter regulations came in.

A deeper analysis of the Le Breton psyche is best described as follows:


## Character

The immediate impression was one of absolute strength. His most striking feature was his direct, forceful, quick-sighted blue-grey eyes. The forehead was open, and he had slightly arched eyebrows, and a clear and firm jaw and chin. With a majestic stature, broad shoulders, his hair was light brown in colour, his voice soft, pleasant and convincing. He was magnanimous in defeat, noble and generous, creative, enthusiastic and a good organiser. Broadminded, he had a sense of showmanship and drama. Honest, upright, and courteous, he had impeccable manners, and was practical and spiritually minded.

He could, from time to time, be interfering, intolerant, dogmatic, even pompous. He also had a rather unique ability to constantly reassess his opinions and he was thus able to use his spontaneous, warm-hearted charm to great effect with utter sincerity. This charm was genuinely affectionate and he displayed a cheerful optimism that really did bring sunshine into the lives of the people who surrounded him, and lightened their daily routines. Ken somehow took this to be his mission in life – it was a valuable quality which he never neglected.

In spite of his desire to succeed, Ken was also very sensitive although when he was feeling hurt by others, he would never show it. No matter how bad the treatment or spiteful the comment, he would always show great self-possession. However, he did not suffer fools gladly.

Ken also had a pronounced flair for the dramatic – while others may have created scenes in order to be the centre of attention, he had a theatrical instinct that could be externalised in more lively, positive ways. Dressing immaculately, everything was done on a grand scale, organising, planning, ensuring those close about him got the best of everything and that the same applied to others who came within his peripheral sphere. While often inclined to be somewhat extravagant, he worked very hard and paid his own way, and was neither in debt nor obligation to anyone, so he set a good example for others to follow.

*Mind*

Le Breton's opinions were formed very early in life and stayed with him all of his days. There are those who say his mind was a closed book, but nothing could be further from the truth. His way of thinking was well advanced, much more than the average person of those times, and he maintained these thoughts stubbornly. He was quite able to grasp and size up the outline of a given scheme or situation around him, far quicker than most other people, and to suggest an even better proposal. He had ideas on a grand scale, sometimes too big, but that was a vital part of his personality. He wasn't the worrying kind. He was often involved in highly intellectual discussions and was much better informed than a great many people supposed.

He was seldom depressed for long, but would crumble quickly when it did hit hard. However, his resilience and powers of recuperation enabled him to recover, and come back better and stronger than ever, shining more brightly and more radiantly than before. Ken's artistic inclination meant that he was easily inspired, and was able to seize upon it, giving more depth, shape and substance to whatever the original idea may have been. His thought processes were highly developed and constructive, and while he was not a sharp thinker, he would still arrive at the right conclusion, by not committing himself until he was sure and positive that it was right for him.

## Relationships

Ken was able to look up to and admire the object of his affection and as such was very loyal and highly affectionate, expressing his true love and complete devotion in a very positive fashion. This had to be returned in a like manner, however. Hate was not part of his make-up; he simply looked upon those who were unable to respond or would not, as a sadness. He loved all creatures, especially dogs, and missed his ever-faithful pets, Darkie and Snap, as well as the family cat (who was an infrequent visitor to the house, on account of the dogs!). Ken never ceased to be amazed at their marvellous devotion and loyalty.

## Career

His natural exuberance and enthusiasm for his chosen work meant that he became deeply involved in it. He threw his heart and soul into it. Work and leisure was one and the same thing. Speedway was his passion — no outside influences or hobbies were allowed to interfere with this over-powerful desire. He disliked amateurs, which made him an excellent teacher, especially with younger teenagers rather than children. He often felt he had his youth taken away from him, and therefore sought to put it back. Ken had a happy knack of being able to goad people into action and he derived a great deal of personal satisfaction from that. He was constantly exploring possible future opportunities.

## Childhood

Growing up, Ken was inclined to be a loner, preferring his own company to that of other children. His parents saw to it, however, that his lively spirit was not curbed. They were also aware that if they criticised him too much, this could dampen his enthusiasm. They encouraged him to improve by showing him how to utilise his standard of behaviour and decorum, manners and demeanour, and to refrain from being too bossy. For a time they worried at his living in a fantasyland with his 'friends', but they put this down to the loss of his younger brothers.

Gradually, these imaginary friends somehow showed Ken how to express himself in certain children's games at which he excelled, but only in those particular games alone. Soon, he learned to accept some of the rules, and would suggest better versions of some of the others. He had it instilled in him though, that school and society rules were supposed to be obeyed, and this would determine his outlook and attitude for the rest of his life. He quickly came to understand that he could be guided by them, and that he could also improve upon them for the betterment of himself and his family – as his mother would say, position and privilege were not only the province of the wealthy and the high born, but were available to anyone who strove to raise themselves to acquire it.


## Education

Ken's early schooling was of a basic standard as taught in Australia in the late 1930s, but inwardly he felt a crying need for enlightenment. He was a slow learner to begin with, but once the subject was digested, he could then expand upon it. He considered reading and writing a boring methodical pursuit which had to be explained in great detail in order for him to take an interest. As soon as the magical flow of words was grasped, however, he became an avid reader. Mathematics was a great puzzle for him for some time. Trigonometry and algebra seemed alien concepts – his idea of sums was to count the number of seagulls sitting on a rooftop!

Fortunately for Ken, he had a teacher who had a vocation for mathematics and he was able to convey the fascination of numbers to his pupils with great ease. Ken's education was further expanded at night school. Whilst in the Forces, this was continued via the compulsory Education Classes that were held. These classes usually meant extra pay for each certificate achieved. Being a Gunner in the Artillery meant that quick thinking was a prerequisite, along with a good knowledge of slide rules, map co-ordinates, angles and computations. It wasn't that he was slow or lazy – he was inclined towards perfection and getting the answers correct the first time round. Besides, being a mechanic meant having a practical application of things mathematical. During his rehabilitation in a military hospital, Ken took advantage of the Government grant and allowances scheme to enable him to go on to higher education courses.


## Interests

While Ken's main interest was mechanics, he was also very keen on the cinema. He was particularly fond of clever actors like Orson Welles, Spencer Tracy, Humphrey Bogart, Henry Fonda, Clark Gable, Bette Davis and Katharine Hepburn. He also liked dance music, jazz and big swing bands. His favourite singers were Bing Crosby, Frank Sinatra, Dick Haymes, Helen Forrest and Hank Williams. He often felt quite honoured to have met some of the top film and variety stars of the day, who were usually invited as guests of honour at speedway meetings around the country to make presentations and perform. His love of all things Scottish was only enhanced by his time living there.

Despite his heavy racing schedule, he read as much as he could, and his tastes varied. He could plough through some real heavy material that took a lot of digesting. He considered Guy Gibson's book *Enemy Coast Ahead* to be a minor classic. He liked nothing better than settling down by the fire with a good book, listening to the radio. On his days off, both he and Joan would also revel in taking in the famous sights on their travels around the country.

## *Personal*

Ken loved health foods long before they became fashionable, and always enjoyed cereals, fruit, rice, honey, and the best cuts of meat. He was very interested in cookery, and was always extremely careful about his diet – he avoided caffeine as much as possible, preferring to stick with fruit juice or milk. On the road, he would eat salads, brown bread and fruit. Reports of him living on a diet of sweet-cakes and sweets are a total fabrication. The cakes he did eat were oatcakes, fig-rolls, malt-loaf, sultana and raisin scones and bran bread. Sandwiches were invariably salad ones, filled with either fish, lean beef, and a mixture of green, raw vegetables such as lettuce, onions and celery. He was always conscientious about his health, and would take plenty of vitamins and avoid greasy meals. It would be fatty foods that were always a temptation in many of the roadside cafés. Such greasy meals were considered an occasional luxury however. Ken also avoided meat pies, pastries and cream.

Ken was a keep-fit fanatic, and enjoyed long-distance runs, gym work, bodybuilding exercises and swimming. He stuck to his fitness programme as rigidly as possible, speedway commitments not withstanding. This enabled him to stay nimble and agile. Whenever possible he would have a good solid eight hours' sleep. Ken had found meditation a great aid in recharging his energies. His life was ordered and organised. A story that has circulated over the years was that he was even referred to as 'Cakey', by certain teammates because of his habit of nibbling at oatcakes. For a brief time, Ken had to endure the sarcasm, until he found its source and dealt with it in his usual quiet but obvious manner.

Le Breton would be a person to avoid if someone was foolish enough to malign him. That he was able to look after and take care of himself was hardly worth mentioning. To have survived a war in the jungle should have been warning enough for anyone, for this required a high level of stamina, great inner and physical strength, let alone a willingness to fight. Ken was around 5ft 9in tall, weighed around 150lbs, and was lean, muscular, extremely fit and light on his feet. Having done his fair share of boxing in the Forces, he wasn't faint-hearted, and had nothing to prove to anyone. He offered nothing but respect and consideration to others, and expected nothing less in return. He could appreciate light fun as much as the next person, except when it went beyond the bounds of propriety and decency. Whenever the conversation or activity stepped over this mark, he would quietly get up and vanish. Anyone who has served in the Forces cannot be considered a prude, for there is very little privacy, but a person can set themselves apart. Nobody needs to tolerate substandard foul invectives and crudeness in their life. Ken would not and did not accept those who pursued such a mode of conduct.

Ken could have moments of controlled anger, when he could fall into a stream of reprehensible curses, usually under his breath, at whatever the current problem to hand might be, but this was an extremely rare occurrence. As a rule, he would stomp off and seek out some quiet spot in the open air, pace up and down, while he worked the stress out of his system. He would meditate until his mind was clear and he was once again back in control of his emotions. Then he would carry on as if nothing had happened.

The one exception was his boredom with life on the road – rattling from place to place, eating habits all awry, shaking hands with dignitaries, signing autographs for strangers, avoiding fights with troublemakers, existing on his nerves with little sleep… the schedule was a punishing one. A demonstration of his talent, which was his emotional sustenance as well as his pride, was often diluted and reduced to mere mechanics by constant repetition. Tempers are apt to snap, so Ken lived on a time plan, which sought the immediate, but the immediacy of creating and delivering can only function in comfortable, familiar surroundings. Perhaps this was why he was content with his current lifestyle as this suited him. To step up to the next level would only increase his stress factor – as it was, he was just able to cope without pushing too hard.

## Five

# BEYOND THE BLUE HORIZON

*I don't see why anybody wants to know about me. There's nothing to me, it's just the image.*

Ken Le Breton, 1949

Legends and myths grow with alarming swiftness around the memory of those who die young, especially in tragic circumstances. Before long, they can become a memory seen through distorting filters, which in the end throw the entire picture out of focus. This, or something very like it, happened in the years following the death of Ken Le Breton. It is not simply that he was held in great personal affection by those who knew him and wished to do all they could in order to perpetuate his memory. It is not even a matter of the esteem in which his colleagues held him as a world-class rider. It is rather a question of substantially extra-personal and non-speedway circumstance, which turned him into what has not unjustly been called a romantic legend in the world of speedway. Hence the 'Death waits at the pits-bend' type of memorial, the sentimentality and dewy-eyed adulation, as well as the reaction against him, especially amongst those who did not fall under his spell and who remained more or less unaffected, simply because in their own personal view he achieved very little.

The situation is by no means uncommon, but it does have an unusual relevance to the present case. Neither of these attitudes – breathless adoration or comprehensive disparagement – is a critical assessment of any value. The one, in fact, often tends to be very much dependent upon the other. The disparagement has arisen to a great extent out of adulation – the adulation of which has reinforced itself against the disparagement. To let in some necessary fresh air, it is therefore first of all essential to clear away the legend, and look for the living man who has become obscured behind it.

If Ken were still alive today, it is doubtful whether he would have been inclined to write an autobiography or even allow a biography to be written. In today's cynical age, one imagines that he would only have been open and honest with those he loved and trusted – his family and close friends. It is true that he had his faults; just like any other person he could feel anger, pique, frustration, annoyance and pain at the injustices meted out. A great many people took to him and felt that somehow they knew him personally, even though they had never actually met him. He represented a generation of young men, who conducted themselves with a proper respect for law and authority, with humble gratitude for their elders, in both private and public life. He evoked a kind of sentimentality which was deeply sincere, and, for those who themselves are sentimental, his loss was almost as hard to bear as was the loss of a beloved husband, brother or son.

In many ways, Ken was an enigma, for he was quite content to sit back and let others form opinions about him, without giving anything away. He could, when necessary, emphasise the point that he had achieved this or that, had done such and such, with little or no help from anyone, and he was able to do so with charm and grace. His humility was plain for all to see. Ken would have surely been World Champion within a few years if he had been prepared to push that little bit further. He didn't claim to be the best, and never bragged about his achievements. By his very nature, even those close to him were unaware of how much he had matured and progressed within himself. Many months of delirium, alternating with meditation and self-analysis, whilst lying on his back in a hospital ward, staring up at a whitewashed ceiling, caused him to re-evaluate his life and his future.

In spite of the latter-day comments, Le Breton was neither arrogant nor big-headed. He realised he was in a cut-throat business that lent itself to back-room politics and skulduggery. This was due to the simple fact that there were more riders for every race than there were places available. Often ability had nothing to do with getting a ride.

At the end of the Second World War, hundreds of thousands of young men went back to civilian life – life that must have seemed somewhat dull and repetitive after the excitement of military life. War is extremely dangerous, but it does provide a high adrenaline rush of excitement. If a person has been subjected to it and is able to come through it more or less emotionally unscathed, then there is bound to be a longing for yet more of the same. Racing speedway is clearly not exactly the same as fighting in a war, but there are similarities in that riders are deliberately putting life and limb in harm's way and taking pot luck on the outcome – the sport offered the scope to satisfy this new craving for danger. To calculate the odds, based on one's own knowledge, expertise and ability, was an entirely different matter. Ken had been left mentally scarred by his war experiences in a way that had forced him to think long and hard about his future.

Coming back to speedway, the one thing he had forgotten was the enormous number of people who were involved behind the scenes. Nearly every one of them seemed to have a level of influence. This was something that seemed vastly different from the pre-war years, when there seemed to be a rather more haphazard, happy-go-lucky attitude at the tracks. Now there were sponsors, dealers in engines, spares, owners, companies, promoters, staff, track personnel and security guards, and big business in every direction. Nearly everyone had to be cautiously approached and gently got round.

It boiled down to Ken watching his P's and Q's, for fear of upsetting someone, especially those from whom he had to beg rides. His father's past connections had long since gone, and would have been of little help in any case. It occurred to him that he might have been accused not of being too shy or reserved, but of lacking personality and not being the kind of rider who would draw a crowd. Given the limited number of rides available, he wasn't sure that he would ever be able to make his mark in his chosen sport.

Honesty, it seemed, was not always the best policy — however, being cunning was! As he had often done in the past, he took some time out and gave the matter long and careful thought. He formulated his plans and began to work on his image, talking and persuading anyone who would care to listen, and writing, phoning and badgering all and sundry, agents and promoters. He quickly found out, however, that there were levels of fame or notoriety. Most sports offer a career with a well-established pattern of progression already in place. However, this did not apply in speedway. It was a case of in at the deep end, sink or swim. The scrutiny was microscopic, and this was to bear down hard on Ken for the rest of his speedway days.

To come up with the 'white image' was nothing new. Many other riders, particularly in pre-war days, adopted some form of colour. Ken remembered the American Motor Cycle Stunt Team that he had seen back in 1937, at the Sydney Show Ground. Part of the show was dirt track-style racing with one rider, Putt Mossman, who appeared all in white including his machine. He was quickly lost amongst that particular brand of circus-style showmanship. That memory stayed with Ken, it was very effective and eye-catching, so he decided to utilise this image. This clash of image and results would have to go hand in hand however. Desperate measures call for drastic action and he simply had to draw attention to himself somehow, so that his performances would get noted and he could then be judged accordingly. Ken was also well aware that a rider was only as good as his last race.

He had to stand out from the crowd. The idea was to win races and to begin climbing the ladder. The name of the game is to win — or is it? Perhaps it was all about showmanship after all. Entertainment: appeal to the public's perception by taking the best of the old and adding it to the new. The concept of all team sports is to win tournaments and championships for the team and the club, this is what the riders and promoters strive for. The ultimate goal and aspiration for the individual rider is to be the World Champion – this is what they all dream of. This is always the case, even when a rider is struggling at the back of the field with a team of no-hopers, the management doesn't have enough capital and crowds are below break-even – hope springs eternal. But with a little luck and the opportunity, talented riders can and do often achieve results that surprise everyone. It then becomes a question of being good enough, and it is believing in one's self that makes all the difference.

This was what he had told himself. The lesson was a simple one. By making slight improvements here and there, perfecting his style and being willing to go that extra mile, the idea of winning, rather than simply finishing, a race becomes ingrained into one's thinking.

When speedway started up again in Australia after the war, the earlier patterns were repeated, with individual meetings and a mixture of solos, sidecars and midget cars. Novices and juniors could get rides on a handicap basis and slowly work their way upwards. This gave them a solid foundation upon which to build their career; not so here in Britain, where the accent was (and still is) on vulture-type races, which have a slight merit, but is more of a hindrance for anyone starting out. This is plainly obvious to anyone who goes to meetings. It seems as though the promoter, or whoever is responsible for holding these races in the first place, says 'let's have one for the crashes!' The track is seldom prepared for novices, but the senior riders always get well prepared surfaces, so how can a novice give of his best when he has an unprepared track to contend with? The insistence of the authorities to ensure the safety of the riders is often not forthcoming in these instances.

In Australia, events are designed with the public in mind, for they feel they are being cheated otherwise, and will not tolerate it. This lesson has apparently never been fully learnt in this country except on very few and rare occasions. Training schools are precisely that, competition is out. So Ken practised whenever and wherever he could, on beaches, gravel pits and waste ground, day and night. It was rough going, with spills, overslides, and much stalling of the engine – he ran through the whole gambit of ill luck and bad fortune, but the simple truth was that there were too many riders chasing too few spots.

Ken made his debut at the Sydney Sports Ground on 17 May 1946. This could be said to be the official beginning of Ken Le Breton's career in speedway, although he had been riding elsewhere in minor novice events prior to this date, beginning with a few rides at the Newcastle Show Ground (Broadmeadow) sometime in late 1945 and early 1946. Now, he found that he was in with top-flight riders, such as Vic Duggan. Ken was spotted off on the twenty-yard ahead mark, but he managed to hold on and win his race, and came second in the final. This was the night that he 'Blanco-ed' his leathers white. (Blanco was a type of waterproof shoe polish used by the military.)

The impact and the reasons for this particular evening are related elsewhere, but suffice to say, this caused a domestic tiff with his fiancée, Joan. She was somewhat put out by Ken using all his savings on second-hand speedway equipment, especially as she thought they were saving for the wedding and to buy a house. However, she was mollified by Ken's success, along with his determination, and was soon persuaded by his promise of an early marriage. Needless to say, as soon as Ken got established he did indeed keep his word, and they were never separated afterwards.

That particular night, and at other subsequent meetings, Ken made people sit up and take note. It is true that many may have thought him a bit of a clown with the white image, and it didn't always work – some nights he came in covered in mud – but there was no doubting his will and resolution. He definitely pulled in the crowds; they hung back at the end of a meeting just to watch him overcome the odds, and the style with which he did it. Often he would let the other riders go, and then he would set about picking them off one at a time, inside or outside. He was calculating, incisive and precise – a real hotshot and one to keep an eye on.

The war had been over for nearly two years by the time Ken arrived in Britain, but the country remained on a war footing to some extent. Britain was heavily involved in maintaining massive troop levels in occupied Germany in apprehension of an imminent Russian assault. Although rebuilding had begun, Britain was still in some disarray; its road and rail structure were falling apart and rationing was still in force (although this decreased with the passage of time). Everything was on a points system, with food, clothing, furniture, bedding, even soap rationed and there was heavy duty tax on practically everything. Black marketeers made a fortune. Whisky, for instance, fetched £5 a quart, while the official price was 25s.

Of course, the war had to be paid for, through the Marshall Plan, which put a further strain on the economy, in order to pay the taxes for it at a time when manpower was short. So the Government kept on bringing in increasingly strict budgets, raising taxes time and time again (including the ludicrous Entertainment Tax, which was to prove a contributing factor in nearly killing-off speedway in the mid-1950s) until it seemed that the only thing that wasn't rationed or taxed was the air itself!

The only compensation was the weather. The summers until 1950 were especially beautiful, with plenty of light until 11.00 p.m. due to the clocks being kept on double-summertime (a legacy from the war). The winters were exceedingly harsh and terribly cold, not helped by the lengthy electricity blackouts. The basic petrol ration was four gallons per month. There was also a shortage of skilled mechanics in garages. The car industry was geared primarily towards the overseas market in order to bring in dollars to offset the national debt. The vehicles in use were either of pre-war vintage or ex-military types.

Accommodation was practically non-existent. Rooms were available, with total strangers sharing, and army cots were used to squeeze in five or six persons. The Government had also commandeered the clothing industry and wool trade in order to kit out recently demobbed ex-servicemen. Sales were much in evidence with regard to ex-military goods. Work was scarce, and National Service claimed the nation's young men to fulfil its commitments. Refugees were a big problem, as was the repatriation of POWs.

Britain's resources in all aspects, financial and material, were so exhausted by the demands of a long and sustained war that there could be no instant return to pre-war pleasurable activities. Getting the country back on its feet demanded that exports came first, to secure the US market. Anything that had to be bought in hard currency, such as crude oil, was severely rationed. The prospects for transport and motoring in general were destined to be bleak for many years to come.

The private motorist's dream of a Sunday drive to visit the local beauty spots was perhaps limited to around a hundred miles per month because of the petrol rationing (if one was able to get hold of some). Despite this limitation, petrol was relatively cheap; the price of a gallon was 2s (10p today) in 1946. As always, there were problems. To import crude oil required tankers, and Britain's tanker fleet was practically non-existent due to the U-boat menace during the war, so they had to be hired; naturally up went the cost. The quality of the petrol after refining was extremely poor, emitting a nasty, foul stench, and with a low octane level of less than 72 per cent. This contributed to the notorious heavy 'smog' in the winter months of the late 1940s.

The vehicles most suited to using this low-octane fuel were ex-military. In every direction and every quarter there were problems of shortages and rationing, with general gloom prevailing. This would last until well into the 1950s. However, speedway required nothing that was rationed. Likewise, any spares, tyres, wheels and frames could be cannibalised from road machines, or pre-war speedway machines could be updated. Leathers and boots could be bought from any of thousands of ex-military stores. There only remained the question of transport. If most of the riders were based locally, a bus would be sufficient. The railway system was intact and reached every corner of the nation – the machines could be easily loaded in the luggage van and wheeled to and from each track. The riders could then catch up on their sleep. Getting decent food and overnight accommodation was the main problem, as was laundry. Those riders who could afford it bought a small V8 car and ripped out the back seat, providing petrol could be acquired of course. Speedway was, as a rule, a Limited Company business and therefore could apply for a petrol coupon allowance.

The people cried out for entertainment, anything to shed the bleakness of daily life. For nearly seven years, they had been denied theatres, cinemas, ball-rooms and sport in particular. Consequently, everything rose in popularity, including the re-emergence of speedway, for it was fresh and exciting and had that hint of danger that people were still used to. Riders of the pre-war years sought to regain their interrupted careers (many, to be blunt, were now past it) so managers and promoters cast their nets far and wide to draw in new talent. It would not come from local youngsters, most of whom were destined for the Forces in any case. Besides which the financial situation nationwide was dreadful. The average wage was around 10s to 15s per week, on a sliding scale for youngsters just leaving school. So unless a youngster had the capital as well as the time, and was willing to risk it in the prevailing eco-nomic situation, he might consider a career in speedway, but few did. Speedway was therefore heavily dependant upon foreign overseas riders. However, while colonials were readily available, continental riders were not, due to the war.

This speedway explosion, which was also equalled overseas (the so-called 'boom years'), created four Leagues with nearly fifty tracks in existence. Tracks opened in the unlikeliest of places, as far apart as St Austell, Hastings, Wombwell and Fleetwood, and, as a result, a large number of riders were therefore required. Overseas riders were encouraged to bring back any new promising prospects, with 'dangled carrots' of return fares, contracts and good prize money. Another plus was the fact that Commonwealth citizens did not have problems with work permits as they had British passports, although a limit upon the number of Commonwealth riders per team was set.

A rider seeking to get established had a very difficult task ahead of him in the late 1940s, for speedway itself was not ready for this expansion. There was little in the way of specialised shops trading in spares, machinery and leathers. As with rationing, things slowly improved with the passage of time, but there were waiting lists for practically everything speedway-related. A JAP engine cost around £75 brand new, for these were easily manufactured and simple enough to produce, but everything else required was obtained on an *ad hoc* basis. A few specialists (usually ex-riders) began to offer a complete rolling chassis for about £200. Again, there was another long waiting list for this.

With the end of the hostilities, the Australian Government gave serious thought to the welfare of its returning servicemen, and their age, length of service and status were all taken into consideration in determining priority for demobilisation. Those who were self-employed could apply for a £500 loan to help re-establish themselves, while those willing to seek a future in farming or agriculture could receive £1,000 to set themselves up. Former soldiers could also apply for a grant to go on to higher education with a weekly grant of £4 10s plus allowances. There were no similar financial grants available to British ex-servicemen.

Anzac servicemen could apply for grants and invest their gratuities and demobilisation pay into seeking a career. Le Breton was no exception, and before long doors began to open for him. He received many plaudits and much encouragement, including a recommendation by fellow Aussies Clem Mitchell and Charlie Spinks, who were acting as talent scouts for various promoters, including Fred Mockford of New Cross speedway. Ken was duly offered a contract.

At the time, New Cross was one of the top speedway teams. All Ken had to do, or so it seemed, was to travel to Britain. After long and careful thought, and much discussion with his father and other UK-based riders, Ken decided to take the opportunity. In those days, the UK and Australian governments were offering cheap one-way fares to emigrants, and for the return voyage the shipping companies sold low-cost return tickets to help offset the expenditure.

On 7 February 1947, with about twelve months' racing behind him and a contract in his pocket, Ken was on his way to what he believed was fame and fortune. He sold up all that he could to raise the necessary capital, made his arrangements, said his goodbyes and set sail beyond the blue horizon. He was in for a very rude awakening.

# Six

# NOT SUCH A JOLLY...

From the moment the tapes flew up, he was in trouble – his first thought was that it was probably something electrical. The drizzle that had hung over the track was now gone, but there was still a dampness in the air. The surface was a sea of wet, sticky mud – it seemed more like an oil slick than a speedway track. Ken had gate 3, always a bad one, for the magnets could not be seen clearly from this position. Numbers 1 and 4 were off like a couple of rockets, with number 2 tucked in close behind. The backspray being thrown up made visibility practically nil, and the conditions were made worse by the front-runners tearing at the rain-soaked surface. The three ahead of him were already rubbing shoulders as they tried to muscle their way to the front, and he had no choice but to follow as fast as he could. Coming out of the second corner of the first bend, he hung his whole body over the white line as he pulled the machine in towards his chest. The front wheel, one inch out from the white line, was so tight that he quickly went past the third placeman, who never even saw him go by.

Now began the race of his life. With his chin practically resting on top of the tank, his body parallel to the frame, his legs forced back by the sheer power of the speed, he chased after the two leaders. Hugging the line ever tighter, he felt the sweat begin to run into the corners of his eyes and start to sting; but he ignored the irritation, twisting the throttle for yet more revs. His machine fought back, determined to go its own way, as it sought a firmer grip on the loose surface. It seemed as though the surface was shifting to throw him off balance, but he would not relent. It was one of those rare days when everything seems to come together.

The leader had twenty yards on him, but the man in second matched the leader move for move, leaving no room or gap – there was no way past. They were not about to give in. Slowly, he gained an inch, then a foot, then five yards; relentlessly he pulled towards them, bend after bend, straight after straight. The spray and slush that had been thrown up for the last three laps still hung there, 6ft above the track, blocking out the overhead lights. The last corner approached, its entry hidden by the two upfront, both of whom took a quick glance over their shoulders at him, sensing danger, and they hugged each other closer in an effort to block any opening. Into the wall of slush he drove, the engine howling like a banshee.

He looked over to one side – the crowd were on their feet, their faces blurred, craning their necks. They watched in awe to see whether he would catch the leaders in time; suddenly they let loose an almighty roar. They saw that he had gone deliberately wide, right out by the fence almost at the midpoint of the bend, nearly running along it, then, for a split second, it seemed as though he had stopped; he abruptly lifted the front wheel, threw the machine to its left and pointed it towards the white line, where it lined up with the straight. Pulling all his weight on the handlebars, he wound the throttle as far back as it would go and shot past the two leaders to win by the width of a tyre. They never even saw him, and those who did wouldn't forget...

This description of a race could quite easily have been part of the screen-play from the novel by Montague Slater for the film *Once a Jolly Swagman*. This was supposedly based upon the life of Vic Huxley, but in the event it por-trayed the life of Tom Farndon of New Cross. However, you could say that the novel was perhaps a combination of both.

The late Bill Owen, who co-starred in the film (Bill was once a second-halfer and a lifelong speedway fan), explained in some detail some of the background to the film:

*The film rights of the novel were bought by the Rank Organisation, and were given to Jack Lee to direct for Wessex Film Corporation. Jack was also a speedway fan from the old days. He suggested that it might have more appeal if the film were brought up to date in keeping with [the] upsurge of current interest. The actual speedway action was shot early on in 1947, when the nights were still dark. This presented a problem right away, as it was being filmed in black and white, how to make the novel translate. Works of fiction are extremely difficult to relay via the screen, for, while in a novel the reader can get inside the character's mind, it takes an actor to bring these feelings into reality. It required actors who were already speedway-minded, and who could handle speedway machines. During the early discussions, it was brought to Jack Lee's attention that New Cross had brought over the latest Australian sensation, some chap who labelled himself the 'White Ghost'. Jack took one look – this was the answer to all his prayers, he would spread the storyline to encompass the pre-war years and the war itself, and bring it up to date.*

*This had been one of the inhibiting factors, in that Farndon had been killed in 1935 and Huxley had retired in 1937, just as speedway was getting interesting and long before the war. Even twelve years later, Tom Farndon was still held in too much rever-ence to touch him in accurate detail. Anyhow, a deal was done with New Cross to film actual races, but as for the storyline, it was plainly obvious to everyone that Le Breton was not up to Division One standard, but he could hold his own with second-halvers, even I could keep pace, as did the others. I don't how much film of actual real races was shot, they had great difficulty with the sound levels, that I do know, so it is my guess, what they covered was a composite of a series of races, then added the studio outtakes with balanced sound effects. They built a track at Elstree, well, the start straight and first bend only, against a black back-drop, I am not sure, but the riders used in the studio may have been Jack Cooley, a few of his mates from West Ham plus some stuntmen. The scriptwriters had long discussions with the New Cross promotion and management, riders, and in particular Ken...*

However, behind the scenes things were not all that jolly, as matters were being taken out of Ken's hands. The impression gained long afterwards, was that Ken had little say or use, or even control, of his image by virtue of his 'contract'. One presupposes that he may have concluded that the consequences of New Cross having signed a contract with the film company was that he would be acknowledged in some part. It is also possible that Ken may have thought he could capitalise on his image factor, once the film came out.

He had arrived in mid-April 1947, coming over with the Duggan Brothers who did what they could for him. Even they were slightly taken aback at the treatment Ken received when he arrived at New Cross. They helped to set him up; Ray sold Ken one of his machines and found him a van. The area close to the track had been badly bombed and was currently in the middle of rebuilding. His accommodation was terrible, very claustrophobic. He had to share a room with total strangers and eat his meals at a communal table; it was rabbit with everything, that much he was able to recall.

So he practically lived at the track, with advice and help from Alf Cole, the chief mechanic, who really took to the shy youngster. Even this caused friction with the other riders, however, resulting in the 'How come Cole helps him and not me?' syndrome. He would spend endless hours trying to master the tiny, tricky bowl. For some reason, he just could not get on with the promoter, Fred Mockford. It always puzzled him why the man kept on demanding references from him – perhaps it was a wind-up? Furthermore, the contract wasn't what he had been promised – there was no guarantee of a return fare for a start. Ken wasn't pleased with the fact that he was expected to provide for himself, and that the other contracted riders had a far better deal than him.

Of course, he immediately realised that they looked upon him as a joke, possibly that the promotion imagined that they had been conned because of his inability to keep pace with the top riders and to get to grips with the circuit. Another added complication was the film company. New Cross had obviously sold them the idea of the image, and they were now fuming at the attention Ken, an untried novice, was receiving. He was between a rock and a hard place, and he hadn't got going yet. He was really up against it. After spending his days at New Cross, working and training, Ken could be found each night at any of the other London tracks, watching, learning, digesting and memorising. Back home, speedway was treated as a kind of day out. Here in Britain it was a real dog-eat-dog situation, and very difficult. Every rider was good, very good – much better than he had been led to believe.

For some reason, Ken just could not get the machine set up the way he wanted it. It needed a lot of work on it and the harder he tried, the more exasperated he got. The image marked him, and soon the sniggers and finger-pointing began. Some of the other riders didn't like the publicity that Ken was receiving. There was much mickey-taking and innuendo. Ken was unhappy, but things seemed to go from bad to worse. The tale of the umbrella man, for instance. This was not a 'stunt' as it was made out to be (although the media writers, perhaps with some prodding, turned it into one). Ken had been invited out to Elstree Studios for a business lunch with the scriptwriter Bill Rose to discuss his possible involvement and input. The few clothes that he had with him were limited to a leather jacket, shirts and slacks – a suit would have to be hired. 'What kind of suit does sir have in mind? A business luncheon. Ah yes, what sir requires is a morning suit.' A morning suit consisting of a black jacket, grey pinstripe trousers and waistcoat were acquired, so off he went. Needless to say, the lunch over-ran, which meant he was late in getting back to the track. With the meeting nearly finished for the evening, there was no time for him to change for his introduction. The evening drizzle meant him carrying an umbrella to keep the hired suit dry. So Ken, being Ken, saw the funny side of it and played along. For a while, the publicity worked, and any publicity was better than none.

It had been a whirlwind of notoriety, as Ken was paraded about and introduced to the high and mighty. However, there was a growing resentment in the background at all this attention he was receiving. There were tiny infractions, such as the odd missing spanner, the slowness of workshop mechanics, his machine being cannibalised for odd spare parts, his parking space being blocked, finding his day clothes flung on the shower floor, a shoe missing, all irritating minor things which added to his discomfort, plus his constant inability to master the tiny New Cross track. His own reticent nature saw him retreating within himself, in order to get to grips with his surroundings. This action, yet again, made him appear aloof and uncommunicative with one and all at New Cross, which in turn only added to his frustrations.

Ken made his debut for the Rangers at Belle Vue, as a reserve, on 3 May 1947, which turned out to be a disaster. Of all the tracks, this was one he could and should have coped and managed with. In his first race, he looped at the gate, was flung onto his back, injuring himself and suffering severe concussion as a result. Returning to New Cross the following day, Ken discovered that filming was in progress, only now there were three riders using his image! What is known, subsequently, was that a heated argument of sorts took place, the reply being that these were employees (hired by the film company); in actual fact they were bona fide riders Jack Cooley, Ron Howes and Frank Lawrence, and others. As Ken was reckoned to be unfit, because of concussion, cover had to be in place for the film company to continue shooting.

A further bone of contention was that New Cross wanted to know why he had been in discussion with other tracks as regarded a transfer! (Ken had been seen talking to Johnnie Hoskins; it was a well-known fact in speedway circles that Hoskins and Mockford had a long-running feud.) Ken was getting slowly angry. By now he realised he was getting the run-around. True there was talk of transfer, none of his doing though! New Cross were indeed seeking to strengthen the team, as they were doing poorly in the League and were scheming in trade-offs. New Cross wanted Bill Longley back; he had been allocated to Odsal. They had also been after Lionel Van Praag, as well as Jeff Lloyd from Newcastle.

Ken redoubled his efforts, only to be accused of hogging the track at the expense of other riders. He now faced a policy of non co-operation from track staff, and arguments about pit space, which was notoriously very restricted, only worsened matters. In spite of this, for his home debut, against Harringay on 7 May, he did quite well; 2 points in one race with two finishes. However the writing was on the wall. To be summarily dismissed, without as much as a by your leave, really irritated him. Snide comments came thick and fast – that Ken was not a team player, spending his time hobnobbing with film stars instead of his fellow riders. Ken clammed up, and took all the backchat and banter in his usual manner, by simply ignoring it.

His subsequent transfer to Newcastle, on 16 May 1947, formed part of what was at that time a record transfer deal of £1,000 for Jeff Lloyd. Lloyd had been nigh-on unbeatable, winning thirty-one out of thirty-eight races, whilst riding for Second Division Newcastle up to this point of the season. Lloyd had stated that he wanted to step-up to the First Division with, preferably, a track nearer his London home. The move for Ken was outside his remit, he had no choice in the matter, as New Cross had now acquired another Australian (Lionel Van Praag), which meant that one would have to leave (as each team was only allowed to use a maximum of three colonial riders).

When he found time later to ponder on it all, a long time afterwards, he told his mechanic, Johnny Duffy, that he was often puzzled why New Cross wanted letters of references, and also why he didn't kick up about the accommodation, which, as well as having to share communal meals with twenty other people, was smelly, noisy and had only one toilet. The thing that Ken detested most, Duffy recalled, was:

*New Cross kept on bringing in other riders, the place was over-run with them at times, Ken always had to go out and try and beat them time and time again. How often did he have to prove himself? There were those who could have spoken up but didn't, and those who did were probably either told to keep quiet or were ignored.*

It is my belief that it was at this juncture that Ken finally 'grew up' emotionally. He had high hopes and placed his faith and trust in those he had previously thought had his interests at heart. It could well be that he may have concluded that he had made the 'big time', landing a secure contract with New Cross, and that perhaps he himself had not been able to handle it all that well. Ken had a much better incentive now. Once bitten, twice shy, third time shame on me, or so the saying goes. Ken mulled it all over and sought the good points, instead of dwelling on the ridicule and humiliation.

Of all the people in speedway who came into Ken's life at this time – and one of Ken's undying beliefs was that the right person would come along at the right moment – was none other than the 'great man' himself, Johnnie Hoskins (the Newcastle promoter). Hoskins took Ken to one side and assured him of his devotion and belief in his future. That noble attitude was to be repaid in kind in the fullness of time. However, at this juncture the transfer took Ken out of the public limelight. He retreated deep within himself, fumed and raged against his fate, until at last he broke out into a series of rashes. Finally, recognising his impotence to do anything about his predicament, he once again sought his spiritual awareness and drew strength from it. So out of the bad had come some good after all. Hoskins found him rooms with a nice, quiet elderly couple that lived locally. They looked after Ken's needs, allowing him to be alone and in comfortable surroundings.

Soon after arriving at Newcastle, Ken sustained a broken foot and was out of speedway for over a month. Ken now had time for reflection, time to get over his disappointments, regroup his thoughts, and, most importantly, time to be able to work on his machinery. Hoskins, being the shrewd man that he was, left Ken alone to work his way back, without the pressure of being in the spotlight all the time. 1947 had been a season to forget, or remember! It had started off brightly, only for it to turn sour. He must have thought about it long and hard. Maybe it had been for the best. New Cross had struggled desperately that year, while the film turned out to be only a moderate success.

By the time it came out early in 1948, Ken was still back home in Australia; it soon made the rounds and was then quickly forgotten. Perhaps the movie industry also lost out, for Ken was as magnetic as any movie star. Who can say whether this might not have been, with the right training and coaching, for the most unlikely of people have managed to become film stars and succeeded in creating a long career for themselves. One such star was none other than Steve McQueen, who started out as a half-mile dirt-track racer himself.

Ken was always totally in control; he knew what he was about. Those people, who go around bad-mouthing others, usually get treated in a like manner. He wasn't going to fall into that trap. So he reapplied himself, got his priorities in order, and set about the business of racing speedway with an unbelievable fervour. Slowly and surely he began to sweep all before him, causing many red faces in certain quarters in the process. If he had been shy and slow in coming forward before, he was now extremely careful in all his dealings. He read everything twice, slowly and methodically, almost child-like, and signed nothing! Every problem and situation was scrutinised in great detail. A massive reappraisal of basic human nature occurred in his thinking and helped him to re-evaluate his approach to life. Quite simply, he had to begin all over again.

Leaving New Cross had been a very bitter pill to swallow. It left a sour taste in his mouth, and was a low point after so many promises and hopes. His father always warned him that if you start at the top there is only one way to go, and that is... Well, he could, and would, show them. It was time for the 'White Ghost' to vanish!

As a point of interest, Ken did indeed drop the 'white image' during the early part of 1948, first going for sky-blue, and then trying a red outfit, but he quickly realised the political statement he was making and returned to riding in white soon after. At this particular time in world history there was a growing anti-Communist feeling throughout the country. The Cold War was beginning to spread, and the Berlin airlift meant that more and more British troops were being sent to Germany to counter the possible threat. This meant that the colour red was out.

All along, Ken had an inner faith and spiritual belief, an intuition that a path had been laid out before him. It was a matter of sticking to his principles and obeying his instincts, of doing the right things at the right time. If someone doesn't believe in themselves, how can he expect others to? It had been a bad start, he knew that. However, it was nothing new, just a step backwards. Ken knew he had got it wrong, had adopted the wrong approach. He simply could not keep up with them. When he first laid eyes on the circuit at New Cross, his heart sank before he even got out on the track. He had correctly guessed that it was going to be difficult to master it, as it had to be broadsided all the way round in practical terms, for four solid laps, and to do that a rider would have to be good.

The motivation was not there; he was a stranger in a strange land. He had somehow lost out, wasn't getting paid properly and was having to fight for every penny. He even had to take odd jobs (such as window cleaning) just to keep going and make ends meet. There was rent to pay, as well as money for food, spares, running costs, transport; he also needed to find the time to train and practise, work on the machinery and sleep. Was he overdoing it? Had he bitten off more than he could chew? A thousand weird and stupid thoughts ran through his mind in those dark days. It had fallen apart – the dreams, the ambitions and the assurances – all gone.

With the transfer, however, came the signs and omens. Newcastle. When he first started racing speedway, it had been at Newcastle in sunny Australia. Several of the riders were fellow Australians that he knew from his days back home. They made him feel like he was wanted and welcome. It was an entirely new world – the people were different and the Geordies see themselves as apart from everyone else. He found them friendly and helpful, and while it was hard to understand the accent, he soon got the gist. They are a people who tell you what they think to your face and quickly recognise a phoney. Before long, Ken began to enjoy his racing again; the hardest part was dropping the image, to get lost in the crowd.

More importantly for Ken, he had found his saviour, mentor and master: Johnnie Hoskins. What Hoskins knew about speedway was well worth listening to, hadn't he practically invented it? The man knew the game inside and out, as well as all the wheeling and dealing that went on. He had seen something in Ken that only someone with great insight, inner faith and a belief in humanity could ever see. Few others could ever match his wisdom. From now on, they both could and would be able to inspire each other.

Johnnie Hoskins' one true asset, which seemed to separate him from everyone else, was his innate and astute instinct to be able to listen to people. It did not matter who the individual might be, but Hoskins would find the time to listen to them and, more importantly, to act upon what had been said. Le Breton's arrival in Newcastle caused a bit of a stir. One look was enough to tell Hoskins that here was someone full of determination and ability who was dedicated enough to reach the top in a very tough profession, but who was also very wary. Ken was conscious of ridicule, but he had the strength of character to rely upon his own endeavours to reach his goals. The fans at Newcastle did not dispute his undoubted ability and talent. It is to their ever-lasting credit that they gave him the time to do so.

There was a lot of strength in Hoskins' and Le Breton's relationship, for they had confidence in each other, which is a rare quality to find in two men from two different generations. Questions of finance and politics are always crucial and it is in everyone's interest if there is a level of solid consistency throughout. Hoskins ensured that this was the case at Newcastle; no one was treated any different from any other. The whole team worked and pulled together, like one big happy family, for Hoskins had that knack of developing and dealing with personalities. His approach with Ken was simply to leave him be. He made sure the rest of the team also followed that thought.

On the personal side, Ken would never voluntarily be pushed into the lime-light, to receive plaudits and trophies, but he soon understood that that was part of the game and his obligation to the supporters. He was aware of his role in these things and would say so. He enjoyed doing it. Ken even went a step fur-ther – he could be found wandering amongst the crowd, chatting to and thank-ing the fans and signing autographs, before and after a meeting. He displayed a shyness, a hesitant reluctance that endeared him to people. His one advantage was that he knew his worth, which made him at ease with his circumstances.

He had a few good friends now, and they liked and believed in him, and so for the moment he was content. He was happy doing what he liked best, racing speedway; that combination of man and machine, with which he conveyed, was very much now in evidence – he had faith, 'total faith', and this was formidable. He could rely upon his own belief and ability, giving himself an edge. He did his own maintenance, trusting no one and relying on his own efforts. He was good, especially when he knew that the others did not have that same edge.

One observation he remarked on was that if he did not like to mix with those (unintelligent!) riders who were quick, then it was better not to do so. Having faith in oneself was fine, but if you are worried about this kind of rider, perhaps then it might be best to quit altogether. His preferred method of dealing with them was simply to leave them standing, as his reflexes and reactions at the gate were lightning quick.

Ken's main apprehension was dealing with journalists and reporters, no doubt a legacy of his time in London. He may have liked some on a personal level, but he was annoyed by the downright-stupid questions they asked – he was quite willing to talk about speedway, but he found all they wanted to talk about was death and women. Ken even said that it was futile inquiry, for, as a rule riders seldom think about death. People imagine they do, but they simply don't. They know when they have been frightened – during a race they can even frighten themselves! Ken never liked that question, was never quite sure how to reply to it. He simply did not have an answer. It would be no good say-ing that he had never thought about it, for that would have been insincere.

1 The master at his trade, Ken wasn't afraid to get his hands dirty!

2 Ken with sister Marie on his father's racing sidecar.

3  Marie, Kathleen and Ken.

4  Marie, Ken and their father, Frank.

5 Ken liked bodybuilding; his father helped him build this apparatus.

6 Ken, aged fifteen with the family 'chevy'. Even as a young man, he was always smartly dressed.

7 Frank Le Breton and passenger – Frank was a noted pre-war sidecar-rider.

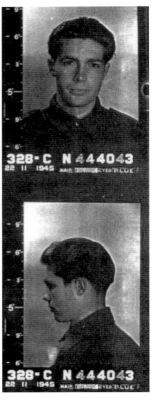

8 Ken saw active service in New Guinea 1943–1945. Here he is on embarkation leave, early 1943.

9 AIF (Australian Infantry Forces) Service ID card.

10 'The trials of dirt tracking!'

11 Ken's first novice race.

12 At the Sports Ground on 7 February 1948. Ken is on the inside (wearing his Newcastle Race jacket) while Bill Rogers is living up to his nickname: Wild!

13 Ken in action at Perry Barr, Birmingham, 8 May 1948, wearing the short-lived red leathers.

14 Newcastle Diamonds 1947. From left to right: Wilf Jay, Alec Grant, Jack Hunt, Johnnie Hoskins, Doug McLachlan, Ken Le Breton, Peter Lloyd, Bonny Waddell. On bike: Norman Evans (Captain).

15 Standing behind Ken's bike. (Note Joan painted on the tank and the colour white back in favour!) Ken with fellow ex-pats Danny Calder, Jack Hunt and Peter Lloyd.

16 Happy in love. Ken and Joan outside the family home in Wangee Road.

*17* Ashfield Giants, 10 May 1949. From left to right, *back row*: Alec Grant, Ken Le Breton, Gruff Garland, Merv Harding, Norman Evans (Captain). *Kneeling*: Willie Wilson, Keith Gurtner, mascot Jimmy Cramb, Rol Stobbart.

*18* First night, 19 April 1949 v Walthamstow. Ready for the parade.

*19* Calm and relaxed (Ashfield, 1949).

20 *Above left* Here's your insurance policy before you try this thing out! Ken and Johnnie Hoskins with the infamous rocket bike (2 August 1949).

21 *Above right* At Sheffield, 1949.

22 *Left* A happy Ken wearing the 'Knight of Speed Trophy', after being presented with it by Hedy Gordon, Secretary of the Ashfield Supporters Club. Ken, ever the gentleman, returns the compliment with a bouquet of flowers. Norrie Isbister is also helping out (10 May 1949).

23 *Below left* Strong sunlight at the first bend, Ashfield. Hence the reason for the long skip on his helmet (summer of 1949).

*24* Jack Young and Ken in the deciding leg of the Scottish Match Race Challenge Cup, held at Glasgow White City on 27 July 1949.

*25* Ashfield v Hanley Potters, 4 April 1950. First meeting of the year, and the heat leaders are discussing their prospects. Left to right: Hanley riders Bill Harris, Les Jenkins and Ken Adams talking to Ken, Keith Gurtner and Merv Harding.

*26* The three Giants – heat leaders Keith Gurtner, Ken Le Breton, and Merv Harding preparing for a special Match Race at Sydney Sports Ground on 27 January 1950.

27 Ashfield side of the pits: Ken can just be seen at the far end. Other Giants in picture are, nearest camera Alec Grant, then Willie Wilson and sitting on his bike is possibly Merv Harding.

28 Ashfield Giants (May 1950). From left to right: Willie Wilson, Johnnie Hoskins, Jimmy Cramb (mascot), Merv Harding, Bill Baird, Alec Grant, Eric Liddell, Bob Lovell, Ken Le Breton, Norrie Isbister. *Kneeling*: Keith Gurtner. This black and white photograph does not do justice to the colours involved.

29 Alec Grant and Ken getting ready for the first race at Glasgow White City, 10 May 1950.

30 Four solid laps, side by side, The White Ghost and The Wasp (Ken and Willie Wilson at their peak at Ashfield, 1950).

31 Ashfield v Cradley Heath (National Trophy Match, 30 May 1950). Heat one: Gil Craven leads Frank Young with Ken hugging the white line. Alec Grant is the rider at the back behind Ken.

32 Norrie Isbister introducing Miss Booth (the Halifax promoter) to Ken before the start of the National Trophy Second Division Final, Ashfield, on 11 July 1950.

33 Ken with friend Vic Duggan prior to their Match race on 13 June 1950.

*34 Above left* Noel Watson who was Ken's protégé and came to Britain in 1950 under Ken's guidance.

*35 Above right* Respective captains Jim Boyd and Ken with special guest, singer Donald Peers (Britain v Overseas at Walthamstow, 25 September 1950).

*36 Right* Ken about to be pushed off for a celebratory lap showing the Silver Helmet (Ashfield, 4 July 1950).

*37 Below right* Team riding with Alec Grant during 1950.

38 All smiles: Joan, Ken, Kathleen (Ken's sister) and Johnnie Hoskins at Ashfield, 26 September 1950.

39 A happy, smiling Ken, with some of his many trophies, 1950.

*40* A lament being played for Ken prior to the opening meeting of the 1951 season at Ashfield, 3 April. Legend has it that it snowed on that day covering the ground with a fine layer.

*41* How people always remember Ken (Walthamstow v Ashfield, National Trophy Semi-Final on 26 June 1950).

*42* Possibly the last picture taken of Ken.

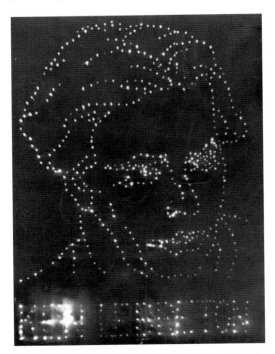

*43* Ken's effigy was displayed in a fantastic tribute during the Interval of the Memorial Trophy in the form of a firework display (Ashfield, October 1951).

*44* Memorial at the family home.

Ken had long since overcome his inhibitions about being inferior and an underdog, and of not being up to the task. He had become a much more balanced person in his outlook, having had to come to grips with himself after leaving New Cross. He showed a modest exterior to the outside world and had his mannerisms well in control. There was now an inner confidence, which told him that he was good, but he kept this emotion firmly in check and to himself. For the rest of his time at Newcastle he worked long and hard. He slowly began to dominate the speedway scene around him, and went home pleased with his efforts and full of optimism. For 1949, however, it was all change – a new team, a new job, a new life, a new country, even a new wife! Maybe now, just this once, he thought, he could be more than jolly, he could be happy.

In spite of many invitations and offers to race at New Cross thereafter, Ken refused to oblige, except when he was compelled to do so. That was twice as a member of the Australian Test Team and once in a World Championship Qualifying Round. Three visits in four years! He was most definitely a man of high principle and long memory...

# Seven

# PRECIOUS MEMORIES

For the first time in his life, Ken now had a reasonable basis of some stability. He was earning and saving money, but was suffering a feeling of loneliness in his personal life. So his thoughts turned towards home and to the girl he had left behind, Joan Minnett, the quiet and well-mannered childhood sweetheart from all those years ago. He had kept in touch throughout the war years and since, sending her letters and postcards of his travels, as well as occasionally talking to her on the phone. There had been an unspoken understanding. Ken respectfully courted her with old-fashioned charm and courtesy.

Many thousands of miles of oceans and continents separated them. To her disappointment and impatience, Joan eventually began to despair and give up hope. Her parents were opposed to their daughter marrying anyone as itinerate, unstable and nomadic a character as Ken, who made his living as a speedway racer of all things! They must have heaved sighs of joy when she let it be known that she was thinking of getting engaged to someone else. As soon as Ken got word of this, his approach was, as always, methodical, practical and immediate. They would get married and Joan would travel with him and act as his manager, secretary and accountant – it made good sense.

Despite the occupational hazards involved in such a lifestyle, marriages such as this need a lot of understanding, patience and trust in order to survive and flourish. Many people have remarked how endearing and enduring was their love for each other. Great credit must surely go to Joan for their happiness. In her own quiet way she was an immensely strong person. She always remained discreetly in the background, yet, when Ken had an important decision to make, he would turn to her and she would help him. Theirs was a relationship of subtle depth – it was said of them that so little was ever said and yet so much felt.

One of Joan's greatest attributes was her ability to understand Ken's moods, of knowing how to cope and deal with them without ever deflating his ego. She was a master of tact and diplomacy, especially good at explaining Ken, and his actions, to others, without ever demeaning her husband. She was extremely warm and considerate to other peoples' feelings, even though she preferred privacy.

One of the nicest, and most relaxed, couples anyone would have cared to have known, they were somehow able to communicate without speaking; each knew the other so well. It was a remarkable relationship; an air of tranquillity and blissful contentment surrounded them. All those who knew them both echo these sentiments – their marriage was one full of warmth, love and simple understanding. Ken brought Joan to Scotland, a land where people have a passion for all things romantic, and they knew true love when they saw it. The couple were totally in love and were inseparable – everyone was pleased for them. A most charming and delightful pair, they were good for each other.

They got married on 8 January 1949 and bought a house close to Ken's old home in nearby Punchbowl, which overlooked a large expanse of lovely gardens and parks, with the thought that within a year or two Ken would be able to retire and build a new life, far away from speedway.

Norrie Isbister looked upon Ken and Joan as part of his own family, and treated them as such. Ken saw Norrie not so much as his boss, but as a father figure – one with whom he could communicate in confidence. Norrie provided a sheltered haven for them both to escape to from the hurly-burly of Ken's ever-increasingly hectic lifestyle.

Because of this, Ken found relaxation in various outlets like gardening and golf. He also became involved with some local charities. He had an inquiring mind, developing his cultural interests as his horizons broadened. Ken often said he was being paid to be a tourist, and advantage was obviously taken, whenever an opportunity arose, to visit and explore art galleries, castles and cathedrals. It didn't matter who the individual might be, Ken could be found chatting comfortably with ministers, police inspectors, politicians, the clergy and tram drivers – and whenever he travelled by train, a visit to the footplate was a must. He always claimed everyone has a story to tell, and all anyone needs do is to listen for a while, that way you can learn so much. Amongst his notations there are a few circled lines. Ken had a fascination for Celtic myths, especially the Arthurian legends. During his stay in Glasgow, he came across the works of the novelist, essayist and poet Robert William Buchanan, the son of a Glasgow tailor, who lived at the turn of the century. The following is an extract that Ken copied: 'Never shall no man speak with me after you, therefore it is for nothing that nay man should seek me out.'

This is not at all that surprising; many students who study ancient Celtic sagas will be drawn towards Buchanan's poems. The poems are based upon the folklore of Merlin, especially those of the Lady of the Lake. Much of it is from medieval French, and this would have drawn Ken's interest because of his memories of his mother telling bedtime stories of 'The Knights of the Round Table' and of his roots. So he was therefore intrigued enough to write down a few lines, especially Buchanan's interpretation of the work of a twelfth-century poet, Marie de France.

> *Far away through the trees*
> *I caught a gleam like moonlit seas*
> *a glassy hint of silvery swells*
> *the lake rimmed round with lily bells*
> *unstirred by rain or breeze*
> *I wandered on, my own to meet*
> *the matchless Lady of the Lake.*

It was maybe because of this and as a memory of his mother, as well as a link to the past, that Ken decorated the rear mudguard of his bikes with the tri-colour flag. As a side-note, Ken used two machines (one long and one short-frame chassis) and each of these was identified by either a vertical or a horizontal motif.

Ken was also a devourer of books, speed reading and then recounting at leisure those which gave him food for thought, especially on the long overnight drives. He would also carry a selection of books in his travel bag. He particularly liked detective stories; Conan Doyle's Sherlock Holmes stories were ideal, for most are short and shrewd-thinking was required, as were Raymond Chandler's Philip Marlowe novels, which he also enjoyed reading. He was fond of totally abstract material, which took his mind away from speedway, and this included a passionate interest in the American Civil War. Newspapers and magazines were given just a cursory glance. Needless to say, he was introduced to Neil Munro's *Para Handy Tales*, an education in themselves, and of course, the renowned William McGonnagal had him in fits of laughter. He liked heavy reading too – Dickens, Tolstoy, R.L. Stevenson were favourites, and classics were a necessity, here he claimed liking Chaucer, Shakespeare, Burns and Scott.

In the early months of 1949, Ken sought out Fergus Anderson for advice and aid (Fergus later went on to become a journalist of some repute and a man destined to become Scotland's first-ever World Champion motorcyclist). Ken was well aware of Fergus's credentials as a top flight mechanic and road racer, and while simple matters such as air-density/carburetion flow, tyre pressures etc., performance of temperamental racing engines in chilly conditions were discussed, so was Ken's flat-out style, which sometimes leant itself more to road racing than the art of broadsiding.

Ken always maintained that everybody knew something that was well worth knowing, and that Fergus knew more than most. It may also have been Fergus Anderson's suggestion that Ken ought to follow his example and perhaps consider writing his own material rather than let others do it, and thereby putting their own slant on matters. Another motorcyclist of note, who was just about to start out on his career and who later came frustratingly close to being World Champion, was Bob McIntyre. It is well known that he sought Ken's advice about taking up speedway.

These insights are provided so that the reader can ponder Le Breton's constant probing into other fields of motorcycling, as opportunities were slowly presenting themselves. Several big companies were scouting for suitable talent for their works teams, in particular, Gilera and AJS, and it is possible to speculate on what could have been if Le Breton had gone down this route. This reinforces the notion that perhaps Ken was thinking about such an endeavour. It could well be that he realised that time was running out for him in speedway, with its cruel, relentless round of constant travelling, for little reward. The average wage was around £25 per home meeting, plus points money, i.e. 15s for a start, plus £1 12s per point. An away meeting was £15 (perhaps with some appearance money added on). Riders had to file for expenses for travel. So the rewards in road racing were obviously much greater, with less travelling involved.

He had a passion for driving, preferring to do the driving himself, but there were times, when he had a full calendar of dates, that Johnny Duffy would accompany him and Joan to share the driving. Ken loved driving at night, especially on long overnight journeys. He wasn't a speed king on the road, compounding his speedway passion, and observed a strict system of do's and don'ts, as he was always very careful about safety, not only for himself but also for the vehicle. He didn't talk a great deal whilst driving, but was constantly thinking and planning ahead. During these long drives, many observations were made and many inspirations felt, and they seemed to come from the concentration the driving itself provided.

This would have been when notes were made, ideas dictated, and lines of thought worked out with his wife, Joan. Ken often mused about the things he had read, and Johnny Duffy explained that Ken would sometimes just ramble on a theme, saying that he had found many things he had been feeling most of his life, without ever quite understanding them. What he had learnt at school now became clearer – the appraisal of situations, what to expect and what not to expect – and he had always believed that nothing was impossible unless it could be proven otherwise. He also found that everyone was capable of making mistakes, and he reasoned that one shouldn't complain at other people's mistakes for they will surely complain about yours.

Ken's senses were highly tuned by now, indicating that he had become a deep thinker. He obviously had some insight as to his purpose in this life – this comes from the conversations that he had with various like-minded people, and it would explain the awakening of his intellect as he sought the answers. His time spent in the Far East during the war would have caused much soul-searching, especially in trying to comprehend what drove the Japanese in their thought processes.

He was also well acquainted with the Aborigines from his own homeland, with a rising awareness of their plight. While many of them had embraced Christianity, the fact that they doggedly clung to their heritage intrigued him.

He inwardly felt that the breakthrough was fast approaching. 1949 was most certainly his best year, he went from strength to strength, scoring maximums galore, and tracks reported their biggest gates when Ashfield were the visitors.

He was breaking track records all over the place; picked at reserve for the Australian Test Team, then to make his riding debut for his country at New Cross (of all places!) on 13 July. Ken must have sensed that this was to be his 'night' to return to the track that hadn't wanted him just a few years before. He had waited a long time for this opportunity and took it with both hands. The Australian Team Captain, Vic Duggan, was out injured; the team were missing his inspiration, and consequently were on their way to a hiding. Ray Duggan, after two rides, had failed to score a point, so the decision to use Ken as a replacement was taken.

First time out, Le Breton seemed very edgy, taking his time, sussing the track out, gaining a third place. In his next race, Heat 10, he was paired with Ron Johnson, against the England duo of Freddie Williams and the old master himself, Jack Parker. Making the gate on Parker, the crowd went wild as Ken held off every challenge from Parker, and, sensing that a shock was on the cards, they cheered him on. After three laps though, Ken's motor started to splutter, and wily old Jack sneaked through to get a lucky win, with Ken hanging grimly on for an anxious second place. He had most definitely arrived! In his next race, the England pairing, Gilbert/Oliver, paid special attention to Ken and crowded him out at the first bend, letting Ron Johnson race away to win easily. Ken got the last laugh though by winning his last race, beating Tommy Price in the process by some distance, ensuring that his place in the Test team was guaranteed for the rest of the series.

The other major highlight of the year had to be his qualifying for the World Final at Wembley in late September (which turned out to be his one and only occasion). Many qualifying rounds were held due to the large number of riders entered in the event. Ken got through to the Championship Round proper, after winning his home round on 5 July at Ashfield, where astonishingly he broke the track record four times in succession. During the next phase of the Championship Round, which was held on Division One tracks, Ken scored enough points to get through to the big night as the fourteenth qualifier.

He went to the World Final practice session at Wembley, shrugging off any dismay at his previous results, which were a roller-coaster series of high and low scores. One day absolutely brilliant, the next he felt that he should not be allowed near a track. For the session he was simply fantastic, and that worried a few of his opponents. He was brimming with confidence and good humour. He followed his usual routine, preparing carefully, but come the big night, he faded, pure and simple, scoring only 4 points. He had this phenomenal talent, yet he seemingly squandered it that evening. Those who were close to him felt his embarrassment keenly. Later on, he tried to explain it: perhaps over-balancing, cross-weighting, wrong gear, track surface kept changing, shorter frame, the handlebars set incorrectly, etc. Ken smiled the silent smile. In truth, he rode like a man who suddenly realised that he didn't want the title after all. Possibly it was a lack of engine power or a slipping clutch, who can now say, but what was apparent was his lack of aggression. All evening his conversation matched his riding, monosyllables and facial contortions. He knew he had got it wrong, admitting as much the following day:

*Well I always said, that if it happened, fine, it happened. If not, life would still be the same. The sun would still be in the same place, and it is.*

A few weeks later, at a private dinner with friends, Ken had this to say about the World Final.

*I gave it everything I could. I was totally empty, drained, inside, you know what I mean. It was an effort. I was a loser for all the world to see. I am sad for Dad. He will be downhearted. It will be hard to get over it, I know that. You cannot have it both ways. Everybody loves a winner. I tell you this. One thing I know. It is not always about winning. You can come across as a real hard so and so, maybe. Or I can be just like everybody else. I am only human you know, and we expose our vulnerability to everyone, the bosses, the other riders, the fans, the whole shooting match.*

As already explained, Ken had previously suffered from malaria. When a person is highly active and full of exertion (quite literally sweating buckets), as is the case when racing speedway, it is not uncommon for those who have been exposed to whatever strain of malaria, to suddenly, and without warning, become drained of all physical energy. The glands have to work overtime due to the body's activity, which allows the fever to gain an upper hand. As the body's blood system heats up the fever is released as sweat, which in turn causes the body to counter-react. The victim is then forced to endure a prolonged period of fever, chills, shakes, sweating, temperature fluctuations etc., which might last ten minutes or longer, and can recur on and off when least expected.

Usually, as a rule, Le Breton was quite able to 'sweat it out', but it would appear as if he succumbed this particular evening to a bout of malaria. His previous schedules prove that he was indeed pushing at the limit of physical endurance, and, as explained, his whole body's immune system was weakened. This then would account for his lethargy. To repeat what Ken himself stated: 'I felt drained.'

A World Championship Final is best described as a weird kind of big game hunting. Over the years since, many different kinds of methods have been brought in to try and supersede the outcome, but do not have that appeal for the public. A one-off world final is a meeting of the fiercest and deadliest form of speedway racing, rider against rider, all evenly matched against his own kind — brave, determined, alert, cunning, stealthy and ruthless — the champion will be an unerring tactician and master of his machine. To deal with it he will have to have total resolve on an impersonal level. The public love it. The sheer physical inner turmoil can quite literally make a rider sick. Indeed some are. All riders throw themselves into it with regard towards none but themselves, mindless of everything, stupid and futile though it might appear.

That night is like no other, every sensation of speedway racing is taken to new heights. The smell alone — oil on hot metal, leathers, the aroma of methanol, burning rubber, sweat — is all prevailing. Here is one pursuit with its own special odour, like new-mown hay, manure, a good malt whiskey, a log fire, or the scent of dew-filled roses. All the riders are aware of it, bound by a common sense of mutual understanding, they share a special bond that no one (unless that person has had that experience) can ever hope to understand. They all know they are risking their lives, of getting injured or worse. Therefore those who indulge in it have a healthy, albeit, unconscious respect for the other riders. Out of this comes a spirit of friendship, which only prevails at times of heightened danger.

Not this night, though, Ken concluded. He was not to share in it. The closest he had come to this feeling in the past was back in the jungle, only then it had been a much more intense friendship, on the very edge of a drop into eternity and hanging on with the last vestiges of his sanity. Then, he had been with his army mates who required nothing of him. On this occasion, however, he was alone. He recalled looking in a mirror at the face staring back at him, belying the appearance he once recalled. He had done and accomplished much. Now the exuberance of his hair was flattened somewhat, his features had sharpened and there were faint lines around his eyes and cheeks. The diffidence apparent in his demeanour, a year or so earlier, had given way to a self-assurance which was evident, even in formal photographs. He could tell by his own reflection that he was nearing the edge; the waves of tiredness would roll over him for a good half hour or more. Perhaps it was a comforting thought that other riders go through the same phase, having their rough moments as well. The risks were easier to cope with in ordinary matches, but a World Final was intolerable. He told himself that the sooner he got back to his own little corner, so much the better. It had been a glimpse of what could have been, the next time he told himself, he would be better prepared.

**Eight**

# THE LOST TALES
# FROM 'ANY OLD WHERE'

This chapter consists of Ken's notations and quotes, written in an abbreviated draft form, for possible future use in the columns and articles. They have basically been left intact, with only minor editing and grammar correction.

– I had 'my' crash. Every rider has to have one bad crash. Broken foot and ankle, strained back muscles, severe abrasions etc., was in and out of hospital for quite a lengthy time. It is a lonely time. It left me feeling pretty weak in physical terms. It takes time to recover, and it has a profound effect upon your thinking while you are lying there for long periods. I would say it is like the bugler blowing reveille, a mental wake-up call. You begin to think more deeply; back in the war your thinking is done for you, it is out of your hands. You make a deal with yourself, your philosophy changes.

– From here on in, the machinery will be A1 all the time, get fit and stay sharp, plenty of rest and proper sleep. I always felt it was morally wrong to take unnecessary risks with one's life, because I believe it is a gift from God, just as suicide is wrong. There are those who say racing speedway is an unnecessary risk. Everyone has a moral responsibility to take reasonable care of themselves. If you crashed, it was in the hands of the Gods, and if you were lucky, you might get away with it, then again, you might not. Obviously nobody wants to get killed or hurt, but the challenge is to race as hard and as fast as possible, while realising the consequences of making a mistake.

– There is also a challenge in knowing that if you are going into the corner faster than the rider in front, but not so fast as to get hurt, then that is a different scenario. Of course, you can try, if you know that the slightest mistake will cost you the race, but not to deliberately take someone out into the fence. There is a creeping lack of discipline amongst a few of the up-and-coming riders, especially on those tracks where there is a catch fence, but on tracks which have solid unforgiving rigid fencing, such as Halifax with its solid steel; Fleetwood, would you believe, [with] corrugated iron roofing sheets,

74

[and] other tracks [which] have railroad sleepers. There is a severe lack of safety regulation, and it leads these unthinking idiots to cause situations simply because of the lack of discipline in themselves. Each track requires different thinking and know-how. During my time in speedway riders have been killed, some of them I knew, it made me feel sad, but it didn't make me change my mind. When a rider gets killed, you tell yourself he made a mistake, nothing more, nothing less. So you concentrate on not making mistakes. If you think you are going to get killed, then it is best not to race at all.

– John S. Hoskins is the most unselfish, the most patient, and the most imperturbable, no matter how dark the day. I am indebted to him for so much of my courage, since I arrived at Newcastle back in '47. He is my listener, my most dependable appraiser, and as a critic he can be the most clinical, for his background shaped him to be the person he now is. His own good taste and understanding is in perfect balance, and that is rare among most men. He developed a theme, an idea, and selected the direction what we all now refer to as speedway, ought to take. I will admit that there were many different kinds of motorcycle racing in years previously, but he instigated its foundation, if you like. Any time I had a debate with myself, about a particular problem or aspect, that may have at some point needed clarification… we would talk, and then the whole world would come into focus. The steady hand of his good judgement pointed to a clear path that suited us both. He is not, as is often referred to, my master, and I am not his pupil. He is my right arm, my left arm, the eyes in the back of my head, my brain waves in his head, and his in mine. Our rapport is the closest. Now, I hope that my representation of him will have the dignity with which he represents me. Many people are indebted to Johnnie Hoskins, and I, more than anybody.

– I have a good, close relationship with many people. I enjoyed my time at Newcastle, the fans and staff there were kind to me, and it was always pleasant to go back there and renew acquaintances. It is difficult to try and explain to people the internal wrangling that goes on in the boardroom. It is a great pity. Pride is a terrible price. Now there is a whole new set-up there and things look brighter now. Here at Ashfield, we have a dedicated crowd of people who are genuinely speedway-minded, and that is half the battle. I have come to know and appreciate as a friend, Norrie Isbister. Not only is he my boss and part owner but a man to listen to. What he doesn't know about speedway is not worth knowing. Just to sit at the same table and to listen to what he has to say is an education in itself. We also have an exchange of minds and it benefits us both. He has been there and done it all.

— It was real speedway back in those early days, those guys had to make it up as they went along, build their own tracks, machines, get people interested, especially the engine manufacturers to develop racing engines. We in speedway today owe a lot to people like Norrie. What he has done here is little short of stupendous. The crowds here at Ashfield must be about the best there are, they appreciate our efforts. Yes, I learnt a lot from him, and I'm still learning. He treats us all as though we are his family, he looks after our interests, sees to our needs, and that applies to everyone, not only the riders, but the staff and stewards, nobody gets overlooked. He has time for everyone whether it's the tea lady or the newest novice. A good friend, and also a remarkable man.

— The curse of commercialism is the ruin of speedway. The charm has gone, and so has the sporting element. Speedway ought to be one of the good things in life, which is how it should be. There are those who scream about the safety measures at some of the tracks, then you get in a race with some of them and they quite happily take you into the fence without a second thought. This is undisciplined. A rider has to have faith in his equipment and trust in his ability. If someone tries to pass, then the idea is to allow him the room to do so. What kind of fellow do you think I am? Respect for the other chap. Commonsense that is all.

— The willingness to admit fear is surely the act of a brave man, sport. I have no time for people who will not help themselves, but it is not the same for those who can't. There is a kind of turmoil; your emotions get jumbled up. Racing has its great moments, but now and then… it happens, it doesn't bother me too much. I lost friends in the Forces too, sure, for a while you grieve for them, everybody does, but you don't suddenly start think about quitting. There is a force that prevails. No one can say what it is, but it is there nonetheless. It has to be. We all love and cherish life and those around us; otherwise we would not be here. I love what I do, but every so often a price has to be paid. Perhaps because of frustration, anger, or boredom, these are bad things to have in your mind. They are likely to get someone killed.

— Half the trick in racing speedway is to know the safe ways of doing so. Intimidate them, what they can't figure out will worry them. Those vulture races, the devil takes the hindmost, then you have to race hard to win, never mind succeed.

— There is no better spectacle than speedway racing under the floodlights, the stands and infield are pitch black, a bright brick red oval with white lines, four riders revving up, the smell of 'fumes' fills the air, while the ears are assaulted by a deep roar of racing engines. There is a kind of special magic in it. To turn the power on and throw the machine sideways into those big sweeping bends, [is] a real kick if there ever was one. A lot of guys have the talent for it, but the good ones somehow never seem to get the chance to realise their potential. You must look elsewhere for that answer. Right from the very beginning, being one of the lads was not for me. I gave up a lot for this. Money isn't the answer, sure it is essential, we live in a material world and we have to have the resources to exist. What I detest are the wealthy playboys, who have never done a day's work in their life, or even served their country, who come in and buy their way up the ladder. It does go on in the sport, as it does elsewhere.

— Safety is paramount; at least [even] those with a pea for a brain can see that. The problem lies with those in authority who have a vested interest. If speedway were a normal business, the Government would take action because of the conflict of interests. They see new money and new opportunities and talent coming along, and they replace whoever they wish whenever it suits them. Referees are sometimes a joke, [as are] rulebooks, [and] pensioners for judges. Who sets the standards? It is much easier to keep quiet about safety.

— There have been many times when I have said to myself, why bother? But if I don't then who will? As long as there are people out there who want to hear the little of what I have to say, fair enough. I hear myself repeating over and over, time again. If someone says it long enough, maybe somebody might start to listen. This is what is needed; a public debate, and surely the supporters up and down the country would like to express their views. If what I am doing pleases them, then I must be doing something right. Speedway is all about emotion, and we inside speedway must be prepared to share that emotion and take it to the fans. If they laugh at it, great! If I can make them feel some respect for the sport, so much the better for us all.

— Speedway has a future, a great future, but it must be run correctly and properly. I am getting paid to do something that I have always wanted to do. So, if you love it, then you will want to share that love. I believe in putting it back into speedway, not for myself, but for the love of speedway. If those who continually seek to take and take, there will be nothing left. Speedway will be treated with disdain, mark my words.

— Military life taught me organisation, routine and order, the best way to function, everything in its place, with plenty to spare. This is the only way to manage things in order to get the best out of yourself. The right frame of mind, no outside influences. Fix your mind and follow the plan you have set for yourself. I stay on top, sharp, on the beam.

— Every race must be planned. Know your opponent, try to get inside their head, watch them at work, study them, and find the best way to deal with them. Likewise, the track. This is crucial. You must know it like the back of your hand. Know where every bump and hole is. Each apex has to be clipped precisely, every exit clean; simplicity and smoothness are the key words here.

— Cause and effect. Think about it. An amateur boxer would no more enter the ring with a World Champion unless he was thoroughly prepared, trained and had acquired the necessary skills to avoid taking a beating. Every action provides a reaction of some sort. You must be aware of it when you are out there. There is not the time to think it out…

— Speedway is part sport, part show business, part entertainment; it is about giving the fans what they want. Good close racing, with everything else added in. They like a bit of rivalry, just like ice hockey, good guys, bad hats. No matter what kind of sport, opposites attract each other. There are many a heated argument behind the scenes as well as in front of the public. No one will sing the praises of another rider, for fear of losing the upper hand or giving something away. Often it is not complimentary either. As time passes, rivalries get worse. Jealousies begin to rise. Preferences take over. The bad-mouthing starts, it gets on your nerves, the constant harping and criticism, sooner or later something snaps. You have to teach yourself to rise above it, for this only leads to problems for both your team and yourself. It comes down to respect. If you respect them, the onus is on them to respect you. I'm afraid, there are a few who are past redemption.

— If the same rider is constantly beating you, then you are more or less finished. Your reputation slips away, and everything that follows just becomes worse. You have to take measures to ensure otherwise. A change is simply the best answer. Various avenues spring to mind. I still try and apply the same logic to what I do and to the way I handle myself.

— The life of a speedway rider is a very stressful one, opportunities to relax are few. If you are not riding, then you are travelling, if not travelling, then you are in the workshop. Perhaps taking an outside job, to make ends meet, or simply catching up on sleep. I find meditation a big help. Outside interests such as writing, reading, study, that sort of thing. You have to retain a sense of proportionality, you cannot let yourself wander off too far, and you still have to keep focused. Staying healthy, keeping fit, eating the right sort of food, a strict regime of planning and thinking ahead. Being over-tired just sets you back, exhaustion, sleep deprivation, leads to carelessness, both on and off the track.

– In a mad world like speedway, to remain sane, one must have a life outside of it. An eye to the future is essential, you only have a limited time within the sport.

– With me, ambition goes in stages. I started with a small ambition, then I built on it, then when I achieved that, I built another. You have to keep reaching upwards. When the disappointments come, as they surely do, then forget them, and do not dwell upon them. Cherish your heart's desire and struggle on to make it come true. I have a secret dream… we all do.

– My attitude for Australia has not changed, it is STILL the best place in the world. Often, I feel Scottish, so I belong here too.

– A lot more riders would win a lot more if they could understand this point, that stamina is essential. Not all track surfaces are the same, some are like a bombsite, and others like a sheet of glass or ice, a few resemble roller coasters or worse. Concentration is everything. You have to devote your mind to the situation that confronts you. I know people think that I am aloof and cold, but that is simply because I have a job to do, and this is how I do it. Concentration drains your mental thinking capacity severely; this is why I prefer solitude in order to recover. To race a machine at high speed, imagine being on a high wire, a knife-edge, you alter the angles and balance by adjusting the throttle and body weight. You have to know what the engine is capable of, and what you yourself are capable of in a required given moment. One mistake and it is gone. You must stay focused.

– Today… everyone has the same engine; only the frames are different, which are built to suit your requirements. Here it becomes technical, power to weight ratios, gears, clutch plate springs, tappets, camshaft, the list goes on. In theory they are all supposed to be the same. However, [as] with every thousandth rifle or gun, it comes out perfect in all respects. So, you have to bring it up to specification yourself. Perhaps the barrel is bored a millimetre too large, or the valve seats are not properly grounded. Once you have a problem, solving [it] usually causes another. Methanol, for instance, is usually supplied by the same petroleum company. It stagnates after storage; this in turn affects the fuel injection. It may be ever so slight, but it can make a difference. Of course, some riders will seek to tamper with the chemical formula with additives etc. Dirt and dust affects the carburettor, fuel tank; air bubbles in the oil system; then there are the spark plugs. As you can see, many and varied problems, how about tyres, pressures, wheel balancing, chains. If it can go wrong, it surely will.

— Retirement? I haven't got going yet. I dare say one day, I will. For the time being, I'm enjoying myself. Though the travelling is a bit much. Best not to think about it too much. One day, I will quit. Always said, give it seven years, and then get out. I have to give thought to my family and the future; this is only a means to secure that. Being involved in speedway is very time consuming. You quite often have to do without the things other people take for granted. A night at the pictures, walks with the dogs, a good book by the fire, weekends visiting the folks, yes, these things we miss. When the time is right, I will know. I'll walk away with no regrets. Then what? Perhaps four-wheels, I do think that motor racing will become really big one day, I am thinking about running a works team for road racing, TT, good prospects there. We'll see. Like everything else in speedway, the golden rule is to make up your own mind and stick to it. There is always someone, who has never ridden a push-bike far less a motorcycle, telling you what to do and say, or that you can't do or say this or that. They may be well meaning, but I am my own master.

— The year always begins with the thought that this will be the year when it all comes together. I have to believe that! You look forward to the new challenges and the rivalries that come with them. Deep down you doubt if you have the ability to make the real big time. You still have to set targets.

— All sports require that you have to practice to stay in shape. It might be long-distance running, golf, cricket, music even, if you can't practice you can't stay in shape, never mind keep up with them. So keeping physically fit is very important. Plenty of track time, endless hours of it. You do not forget how to ride a motorcycle overnight, but you do know within yourself when you are not well and not in shape. There comes a time when you can push too hard and it will fall apart. Working on engines is often a case of little things done often but better. Figuring out exactly what is best, so do not accept blind faith, until it is the way you want it. It is more often just a feeling than anything else. While there are adjustments to be made, usually it is how fast will the machine run. A timed flat straight run over a mile (an old airfield is better than the beach, side roads are out of bounds, too dangerous).

– When problems occur, you have to find the cause. Start with yourself, get your mind fit and organised. Contractual and money problems are the basic root, sort out the finances and go from there. The worst thing is, when you think everything is all right, the machine is running smoothly, then you come in and check the times, and you find you have been crawling round. You then begin to worry and get frustrated and anxious. The way it works is that you become familiar with everything that goes on with the machine, and how it has to respond to all the different kinds of situations that come along. Ideally, to be the best, is to have a brand-new machine for every race, but who can afford that? The day will come when that will happen! So it comes down to the rider himself. He and he alone has to sort out all the problems, slowly and methodically; you live it, sleep with it, day in, day out. You have to know each nut and bolt, the strongest and weakest points, how much stress, how each part works in conjunction with its neighbour. Make small changes one step at a time, very time consuming, but, slowly and surely, you work out what is best. It does work that way – anything less and your morale and confidence will have vanished completely.

– Being team captain also means that it is my responsibility to reassure others of their shortcomings. To suggest possible ideas and probable answers. Try to keep them motivated when their prospects are looking bleak. What I do is to use my own disappointments and illustrate my particular problems, but this is apt to lay you open to criticism, for they can then turn the blame on you for their failures. Everybody should look for improvement, starting with themselves, for they will be the first to assess their own performances. If it works for them, this then conveys the message to all the others.

– A riders' particular riding style is a totally individual thing. It is like handwriting, because your riding style is merely an extension of your personality. Most ride in subtle, slightly different ways from everyone else. Hence it is extremely difficult to teach someone how to ride. True, the basics can be taught and shown, but to really master the craft can, and often does, take several years to get to grips with. To become an accomplished rider, one has to have some talent for it. While there are those who quickly acquire the knack earlier than others, by virtue of starting early they will burn out at an early stage. On the other hand, if they proceed slowly at their own pace and work their way up, gradually, it will all come together and fall into place. For these individuals will have worked out their own style, and therefore use it to greater effect to suit their own needs, and will have a longer career as a result.

– Riding speedway is a science. The corners are not tackled aggressively, there is a learning process that demands the blending of turning/accelerating into a smooth action whereby the machine is taken to its limit, if need be! There is a need to find out what that limit is, of course. So good riders first analyse their riding habits to see where they can improve; this way they can keep going, barring injuries, for many, many years.

– Then there are the 'jumbucks'. These fellows really have to graft hard at it. They may look spectacular, but they are all over the place. This is neither good speedway nor is it good teamwork, though a shrewd promoter will seek to include a few in the squad, just for that reason alone. Here lies the problem. To win things means an all round 'smooth kind of rider' who can combine with his partner, without any acrimony. To help and guide each other to achieve results. Or have a team of 'wild-ones', against whom no other rider will risk his life. They are not fast, they forget the line and balance, they simply do not think. The art of speedway is about juggling all the different factors and forces, the type and make-up of tracks, how to balance and be sensitive to the situation of the other riders. There isn't a right way or a wrong way, it is a question of abilities and machines.

– It is human nature to be stubborn, and nobody likes to be told what to do. A rider with bad habits is pretty much like a golfer with a bad swing. Some will try hard and learn. Others will listen and strive to find that edge, so they can improve. It takes a lot of nerve to heel a machine at a precarious angle and turn the power on. Concentration and determination. Having complete faith in the other chap's ability. Each is seeking that racing line in order to get the drive. You have to think, watch, search for the slightest of advantages, making compromises. Your machine has to be properly set up, balanced, responsive. You must feel comfortable in the corners, with plenty of power for the straights, regardless of the conditions.

– How long will an engine last? Until it falls apart is the answer. It could blow after being revved up, or it could collapse after ten yards, it is hard to predict. I have tested engines to destruction, lap after lap, stopping only to top with fuel/oil, till it goes. Then you set to work, examining, testing, measuring for wear and tear, and seeking the weakest parts. The whole machine in its entirety. This is where it counts, off the track, in some cold workshop, there the real work begins. I can take an engine to bits and rebuild it. In time, perhaps I could build a better mousetrap, as they say. I know what goes on inside, I know the points of stress the machine will accept. You have to have a feel for such things. Jack Teagarden, the trombonist, he could build you a steam calliope, not many could do that. He is a very gifted musician, and he could construct musical patterns just as easily. Get the point: I love taking things to bits and rebuilding them.

– My Dad and I share the same fascination for mechanical things, but I learned a lot in the army, there you had to be innovative as well. So I do much of the work myself; if something goes wrong I need to know how to solve whatever the problem [is] that arises. Mistakes are made, and can be costly, but what you learn is priceless, and there is the satisfaction of doing something by yourself and getting it right. I also know the anger and frustration that comes from mechanical failures. These engines are very temperamental at the best of times, they seem to have a life of their own… and they act up when you least expect it.

– Ever since I was a child, I have had a passing interest in the Bible and spiritual matters. I have often said, each time you read a portion of it, you learn a little something, or perhaps suddenly understand something I had already learnt. I will be honest and say this much: to have been in a war situation shakes a man's faith in the Almighty. Just look at the misery war causes. We, all of us, have to try and do better. It seems that there is always some dedicated soul who seeks me out, or sometimes I seek them out, perhaps folks come visiting and something will get said in the conversation that helps illuminate the path. I have lived in the Far East; take it from me, that kind of experience alters one's thinking. Christianity is one of the newer religions, them fellas (Aborigines) back home have been around for ages, and they know far more about God and all that religious stuff than any of us will ever do. I believe each of us has to find God in his own way. If you don't believe me, some moonless night have a look at the night sky, that will make you think. That is all I have to say on the subject.

## Nine

# MORE ONE CANNOT BE

When Ken Le Breton passed away on 6 January 1951, circumstances gave a special twist to the sad news which made the headlines of newspapers on either side of the world, both in Australia and here in Britain. The speedway media themselves were stunned at the news, and were unable to adequately respond until later.

Le Breton was barely twenty-six years old; active, and in heavy demand, he was as popular as ever. He was busy broadening his appeal still further; newer and more lucrative avenues were on the horizon, and a lot of focus and interest was being turned in his direction. The curtains were about to rise upon a new bright shining star.

Ken's death was the loss not only of a man, but of the championships and titles he would have undoubtedly gone on to garner. The manner of his death evoked both an admiration and a deep respect, adding to the brave image of Le Breton himself. Of all the great speedway stars of those superb 'boom-years' of the late 1940s, Le Breton was not the first to go. True there were other special cases, but the jolt and realisation about the mortality of the man, and a very likeable one at that, caused many people to search their souls. Cynics and agnostics, Christian believers and speedway lovers, none were excluded.

None of these factors weigh much consideration beside the fact that Ken Le Breton deserves to be remembered for the fine and sensitive person that he was. It is not necessary to embrace the simple-minded adulation of the fans and for the image-makers to respond warmly to his particular qualities as a performer and to find a topical relevance in his style.

Of course, luck played its part. Although stardom had come late to Le Breton, it gave him sufficient time to develop and to display his persona to greater effect. Other riders before and since have gained more and achieved greater glories, but it is a truism to state that none were (or are) as brilliant and possibly so long remembered.

The public are very selective about what they respond to, and, mostly and understandably, it is those great colourful pioneers from the past who are still warmly retained in peoples' memories today. At other times within speedway circles, and for many different reasons, there may be a need for cynicism, brashness, cruel hard-headedness, coldness and ruthlessness. However, these cynical individuals and their snide remarks are soon quickly forgotten.

Le Breton was a man confronted with danger early in his life, and this seemed to stamp him as a vulnerable figure, one who might succumb at any given moment. So what kind of person was he? It all depends upon on who one talks to. Nearly everybody has an opinion. Some have said he was a man of volatile temperament and violent inner impulses; others again say he was a sanguine type of fellow. It is his response to the inner stress, as well as the outside danger, which grabs the attention. Perhaps his neurotic touchiness and his clammed-up aloofness (he disliked total strangers to touch him for instance), reflected a profound disillusionment and disenchantment. So, Le Breton has our sympathy rather than our condemnation for these minor flaws in his character.

He drew an emotional honesty and a deep commitment from those around him. It seems as though there was no happy solution, only more living to be done with as much style as possible. A modern dilemma: a model hero in the midst of crazy, muddled and dangerous times.

His particular effectiveness as a star in the making began with his features. Early photographs are hard to believe, they show a debonair young man with a striking smile and uncomplicated features. A slim, quiet and charming man, his handsome looks display a 'character' that had experienced life and was hardened by most of what he had seen. This was an image that he worked on, much as an actor might. He played on his facial aberrations – the tightening of the eyes, sucking in of his lips at moments of stress or annoyance, portraying a haughtiness, licking his lips, a stare so penetrating that one could feel it reach into their soul – all of which made his face one to watch.

Le Breton had a vain side also. He liked to be well dressed; he was clothes conscious, always clean-shaven and immaculately groomed from head to foot. He accepted that his working life was one full of dirt and grime, but even here he constantly appeared clean and smartly turned out. His voice was soft and quiet, he spoke clean and fast, after a long pause for thought first, and then forcibly and often at a dizzy rate. He could mimic with ease and with humour, and he found that the easiest way to get on with others was to be able to answer in a like manner. He appreciated the finer things in life, great art, books and paintings, sculptures, gardens full of flowers, and he tried to surround himself with them.

His actions and reactions were usually carefully considered; only under extreme provocation did he ever blow his top. Another skill he had acquired was in the art of listening, which is easier said than done, and he knew how to also ensure that a person was listening to him. He had developed, with care, tiny mannerisms such as brushing his lower lip with a fingertip, or playing with an ear lobe, or perhaps pushing an imaginary hair away from his eyebrow, or sometimes stroking his chin thoughtfully. These actions may have been seen as spontaneous and accidental, but these little physical tricks were calculated to ensure that he had the listener under control. Astute, alert, adept and clever with words, he knew how to make his point. Only those who were very close to him knew how hard he had worked to draw himself up out of hard beginnings,

His private life somehow added to his lustre as a star. He was publicity conscious, and understood the value of a good press. He was nobody's fool, and would not tolerate trite nonsense from reporters and pseudo-journalists. The media liked Le Breton, for they knew he could be relied upon to provide stimulating views upon almost any subject, and to show a little disrespect to the hierarchy within speedway, highlighting their faults at the way speedway was being run.

Those who worked alongside Le Breton attest to his utter professionalism. He came totally prepared, nothing was left to chance. At many meetings he would loan his machines to his teammates, in order to encourage them to follow his doctrines. He detested amateurs, improvisers and Mickey Mouse operations. He had strictly defined views about speedway, and would have no hesitation in saying so.

Le Breton had no political beliefs *per se*, though one suspects he might be classed as a Liberal devoted to democracy, criticising those who sought to demean those who were unable to speak upon their own defence. As a young man he had to fend for himself, as many other young eighteen year olds had to in time of war. He had also known hard times within his family days, when there may have just been potato soup on the table and nothing else. He had learned early to grow up and fast. He soon found the value of friendships and what it meant to be respected. Life in the Forces is a great leveller of ideals and thoughts. He kept his own counsel and sharpened his wits. He was muscular enough to be able to look after himself and not to be put upon.

Like most people, Le Breton didn't like being talked about, saying that it was a 'fair cow'. He certainly did not like being written about either, believing that any sort of written tribute was little short of an obituary – unless he himself had written or sanctioned the writing! The conclusion was that he was a rather modest person. However, the truth is further than that, for he had given a great deal of long, hard methodical and logical thought to the possible outcome of any involvement in any publicity, be it a stunt or genuine sports reporting, and the resulting interest thereof. He was quite able to do his own talking and to ensure that whatever was used was to his advantage. He could, with consummate ease, expound and evaluate themes, and generally expanded upon ideas and schemes as to how speedway ought to develop.

Le Breton acted and behaved as though he was a bit of a genius, which confirms our long-held view that in all probability he truly was. Everything he said or did was very nearly achieved, and adds up to the fact that he really did give speedway that vital jolt at the right moment. He knew what the sport needed; he just needed others, particularly those in authority, to see it too. What he sought was a figure of such standing, but who was also someone of like mind, and this he found in the person of Johnnie Hoskins.

Aficionados of speedway folklore can truly wonder at the eventual outcome of these two people. In recent years, other notable riders have, in their own way, sought to exploit their endeavours, for the betterment of speedway, and singularly failed to do so. It could be argued that, perhaps, they lacked the wisdom of a figure such as Johnnie Hoskins behind them.

Ken Le Breton scorned critics and writers, a trait he shared with many other top sportsmen from whatever corner of the globe they come (then and since). He was extremely careful, though, to be politeness itself whenever he had to deal with the media. There are critics that other critics do not like either, so it would be unfair to say that he dismissed them entirely. The early writers of speedway built up the sport and created images that gradually took away the circus-type flavour, aided and abetted by the riders themselves, elevating the standards. They were succeeded by younger and more enthusiastic writers, who raised many a mediocrity into a myth by some stint of hard writing.

The pop music mentality that became the norm in the late 1960s can be compared to speedway of recent years, whereby riders are similarly manufactured because of their wealth and not their talent. The riders of pre-war and immediate post-war were compelled to rely upon their talent and skill. Le Breton, a remarkable person to begin with quite apart from his natural gifts and talents, would have soon been noticed without the help from any journalist. He just had to make them aware of him, and he knew how to do it.

When a man becomes a legend, it is only to be expected that some of the facts of his life will become expanded, to make a greater impression upon the public's fascination with that man, especially in a sport that was – and still is – starved of 'real' stars. Le Breton may have been a little guilty in stretching the truth at times, and of possibly inventing a few stories, but that is only human.

In common with most other young men, he loved the sense of speed, which for him became the be all and end all. Perhaps he tried to hide his adventurous boldness at taking risks, which may have led to him often becoming misunderstood and viewed as a man of mystery, aloof and cold, made of stone. Tales of the police seeking a phantom riding a high-powered motorcycle with no lights and silencer, along highways in the middle of the night, may or may not be attributed to Le Breton. There is a grain of truth in it somewhere, for he certainly kept very quiet about things like that when questioned. This was the kind of story to which he would smile his silent smile and leave open to conjecture.

It is always easy to take the mickey out of what the majority consider to be outside the norm. Le Breton's secret was his ability to laugh at himself. Conducting interviews was his forte, and he could be extremely cutting whenever the need arose. If some acid-type of correspondent demanded an audience, he would be all obliging and subservient, replying mildly, 'By all means, now then what time shall we say? The meeting starts at 7.30, correct? Then 8 o'clock will be fine!' Or he might confidentially 'reveal' a story to these inquisitors. A classic one was of his plans for the future, to run a garage operated by girls on roller skates as petrol attendants! He relished telling that one.

A born performer, he had his need to be the centre of attraction, brilliant in front of the paying public. He excelled in this. Debating with hard-nosed businessmen, or simply holding court with his fellow competitors, he was in his element. Many people who are like that can be, and usually are, insuffer-able, but Le Breton was a truly genuine and very likeable person, to whom nearly everybody responded with equal ease, enthusiasm and loveable affec-tion. Had he lived, one could imagine him being rather like David Niven, a regular invite on chat shows, with a fund of humorous stories. Perhaps a mod-ern comparison might well be actor and fellow Australian Russell Crowe; he too has that kind of mannerism that charms people from all walks of life, as well as attracting critics!

Le Breton's concentration was such that if anyone spoke to him, he would often claim that he had never heard what had been said. His talent was unforced, it flowed with an ease that left others in awe at what they had just witnessed. He worked hard at it, though, and would come in after a race drip-ping with sweat. His opinions scarcely matched the then contemporary thinking to be found in the speedway pits. They came from a highly intelli-gent and extremely rational individual who had clearly thought about the dangers, and had analysed, measured and accepted the inherent risks. Here was no wild, carefree abandon, no bomb-happy merchant at work, but a cool, calculating, clear-headed rationale in operation, very deliberate in the execu-tion of the task laid before him.

Ken was a very hard but extremely fair and determined racer, one who used his head. If he could win he would do so, but if it meant a third spot then so be it, for he could apply the same criterion to that task as well. Le Breton was the ultimate sportsman: analytical, invariably calm, with no sign of emotion. He was one of those elite band who could be seen constantly reaching beyond the accepted limits. In a bear pit akin to the Roman Colosseum, riders preparing to wage hatred and carnage upon their fellow riders, Le Breton appeared majestically head and shoulders above all the bedlam and hubbub, quiet, unruffled, seeking not to lower himself to the baser levels of his competitors. True he had his share of critics; he had been sneered at, ridiculed, humiliated, sworn at, threatened with violence and even laughed at. He endured the innuendoes with humility, though it didn't sit easy with him – he could have been like the others and lashed out, verbally or with fisticuffs, but he didn't. He could have been one of the boys, but he was better than that; somehow he felt he was destined for a greater glory, that there was an unseen hand guiding him.

Of all the many statements gathered, this one particular theme keeps repeating itself: a strange, quiet, distant young man assured of his place and destiny.

Le Breton owed so much to those who had faith and belief in him, those who shared the same thoughts and agreed with his principles. They knew of his sacrifices, of what he had endured, and they also knew of the long suffering and hard physical labour in order to raise the means and capital to sustain himself. He had proved to himself he wasn't a coward. He had served his country loyally and proudly, worked hard and paid his taxes like any other citizen. He asked for nothing that was not his by right; as for the rest, he only asked for the opportunity to earn his way.

There have been better and greater riders before Le Breton came along, and many more since, but few have captured the imagination and interest of speedway supporters as he has done. On his day, he was capable of supreme greatness, and fans never knew whether a particular day might be just one of them. A day without racing, he once remarked, was a day lost. Like all truly great riders, he had no need to brag about himself.

Le Breton had a very distinctive style of riding, very precise and accurate. He excelled at gating, leading from the front, and, from that position, it was near on impossible for anyone to pass him, far less stay in front of him. It wouldn't be unusual for that rider to then be preoccupied with staying there, unsure, perhaps, about how hard to keep pushing, for Le Breton was also a master of attacking from a long way behind. When in front, Le Breton was in control of the race. He would slow his pace to match the following riders and then his flat-out style of riding came into its own. He would crouch low over the tank, his spine parallel to the frame, the bulk of his body over the rear wheel, elbows tucked in, and his arms pulling down hard on the handlebars.

More often than not, his gating was *par excellence*, no matter from which position, and this superiority freed him from the usual dogfight behind him.

His reactions and reflexes were razor sharp and he had the eyes of an eagle. He would slot the machine to gain the merest glimpse of the gate magnets; his balance was that of a ballet dancer. Where other riders relied upon power, Le Breton had some kind of sixth sense that aided him, for he was able to time his co-ordination of clutch/throttle control and hold and steer a long straight course, before having to make any adjustments.

There are those who say only winning matters, but it was more the way that Le Breton won his races — by imperious command. His style may have been flamboyant, but only when he had to be, generally there was never any need. He was simply a born racer, relaxed and smooth, inch-perfect on the white line, lap after lap, reflecting his orderly and logical approach to speed-way. When the need arose, he could play second fiddle with consummate ease, taking the hardest riding line, and shepherding his teammate home. Or he could block the riding line and slow the pace to suit. He may have taken his pleasures simply, calm and serene, but the second the goggles were slipped on a change occurred — the warm, friendly, sparkling eyes suddenly became flints of cold steel, very, very intense.

The Sydney Sports Ground triggers a lot of unhappy memories; in a way perhaps it is best that it is now no more after the loss of so many lives there. The local press reports on that fateful day simply state 'Le Breton killed' in the sports columns. It did seem unlikely that they should dismiss such a great talent with a mere handful of words. However other, far more important, horrors were filling the newspapers and dominating peoples' thoughts, such as the high casualties from the Korean War and talk of nuclear weapons possibly having to be used. The sudden death of a sportsman consequently did not rate high. Yet still there were a few vain hopes that it was another with the same name, per-haps a mistake, and for a little while there did indeed appear to be some doubt.

At that time news from down under was often slow in arriving in Britain, but, once the doubt became a fact, the news hit the headlines in all the national newspapers, especially in Scotland and Glasgow in particular, where Le Breton was considered to be one of their own. The street bustle of busy Sydney was stilled on the day of his funeral. Along the straight highways a mile-long cortege made its way, escorted by police outriders, to the crema-torium at Woronora. Thousands of people lined the streets and paid silent hom-age, many with tears in their eyes. In the days that followed, the media sought explanations for the accident; much was made of a supposed feud, and of pos-sible premonitions and superstitions.

There is no denying that during those last few weeks there did appear to be a strange new desperation in Ken's riding. Here was a rider well versed in his craft, with a mechanical know-how that surpassed many of his colleagues, and yet he somehow seemed to be desperately alone, unable to get to grips with his speedway. An air of melancholy sadness prevailed in his presence. He appeared to be uptight, often difficult to communicate with, obviously preoccupied, and fretted increasingly. Away from speedway circles he talked to those close to him about the hassle, and of perhaps quitting the sport before too long.

It says much for his ingenious character that he retained his devastating drive and force at previous meetings prior to the Sports Ground Test Match. There is no possibility at this late stage to determine the true facts, but it does seem as though he was depressed, and this affected him. It was a tension of sorts, possibly amplified by recent poor results. Many have attributed this as a contributing factor. However, Le Breton was never one to show or give way to much emotion at the best of times, and doubtless he may have covered his fears and uncertainties with his usual flair and regard for putting on a show for the fans.

What is known is that he hardly spoke that particular day, except to remark that he felt a bit tired and weary. Those who did speak of it remarked that they felt a kind of presence around him, something in the air. There was nothing false about Le Breton, whatever it was that he may have felt was kept very much to himself. Photographs of him that last evening show him apparently happy and smiling, acknowledging the crowd. As always he stood out from the other riders, but here he seems to even more so.

Jim Shepherd, one of Australia's leading speedway journalists and eminent historian, explains the events of that night.

*Friday, 5 January 1951 to be exact – but my memories of Ken Le Breton's fatal accident are still vivid enough.*

*There are some people who were at the old Sydney Sports Ground track that night for the second Australia v England Test Match of the 1950/51 series who disagree with my recollections, but I still believe I had one big advantage. That night I watched the fateful race from the Press box, situated high up and next to the main grandstand, just past the finish line. From that position, although removed from the intimacy of the action, I was afforded a panoramic view of the track. Those who watched the race closer to the safety fence, or the crowded confines of the pits, halfway down the back straight, had a restricted view because in that era spectators were allowed to sit hard-up against the safety fence and were continually ducking the flying dirt.*

*A myth – and that is what it remains – which grew up around the accident is that England's Eddie Rigg 'deliberately' rode Le Breton high on the final bend, forcing him to crash into the fence. The myth had its beginnings linked to an incident involving Rigg and Le Breton in the First Test at the old Sydney Show Ground track on [one] Saturday night, 16 December 1950. In Heat 3 of that match, Le Breton tried hard to force an inside pass on Rigg and the Englishman twice had his leg caught in Le*

*Breton's machine. After that race, Le Breton was cautioned by the steward for 'over aggressive' riding. Ken was in an aggressive mood that night; scoring 11 points in Australia's easy 63-45 win over the tourists.*

*Rigg and Le Breton shaped up again on 22 December in the New South Wales Championship at the Sydney Sports Ground, but on that occasion there were no fireworks. Rigg rode well to score 10 points, Ken had a lacklustre night and scored only 8 points, and the championship was won by Jack Parker with an unbeaten 15 points.*

*The next time Rigg and Le Breton faced each other was in the Second Test on 5 January. The accident occurred on the final bend of the final heat. Australia's Jack Gates led all the way from the start from England's Bob Fletcher. Rigg and Le Breton, who missed the start, were tailed off. All four riders were well spaced until the start of the final lap when Le Breton began to close a little on Rigg.*

*Entering the first and second turns, then known as the Moore Park bend, Le Breton moved to centre track and poured it on down the back straight. Going into the third corner and about halfway through what was then known as Paddington Bend, Le Breton moved a little higher and edged closer to Rigg's rear wheel. From my high position looking down on the bend, I was convinced that Rigg, who was roughly centre track, did not change his line. Ken must have thought he could take Rigg on the outside and moved a little higher towards the fence.*

*It was all over in a split second. Ken's front wheel collected Rigg's rear wheel and Ken was pitched sideways to his right straight into the hardboard fence. Rigg was hit so hard he was pitched over the front of his machine. Ken didn't move, but Rigg struggled to his feet and began limping back towards where Le Breton lay. A flag marshal was the first to reach Le Breton, just ahead of the ambulance, which sped to the scene from the centre green.*

*Few present English fans would know anything about the old Sydney Sports Ground track, so it is worth pointing out that the 418-yard circuit, built by Frank Arthur in the late 1930s, was of uniform shape, but had at least one peculiarity. The track was gently banked to about the midpoint of the 30ft width, but from the centre track to the safety fence, the banking tapered off and the track was virtually flat high up near the fence. The higher a solo rider went on either bend, the more he slid to his right, because he was coming off a slight banking onto the near horizontal. The high line Le Breton appeared to be taking on the final bend was never going to work.*

*And therein lies a mystery. His last lap charge on Rigg had worked to a point where he had closed the gap, and the obvious passing line was on the inside of Rigg. Remember also that the tight inside line passing was a Ken Le Breton trademark everywhere he rode. Completely forgotten now is that both Rigg and Jack Gates were pallbearers at Ken Le Breton's funeral. So much for the Rigg-Le Breton 'feud'.*

*The man closest to Le Breton on the night of the accident was his riding partner Gates, who is adamant that he cannot recall any ill-feeling or any form of aggression between the English and Australian riders in the pits – and the Sydney Sports Ground pits were so cramped that rivals continually brushed up against each other. What he clearly remembers, however, is that several times Le Breton said he was feeling very tired that night. When the pair walked out onto the track before that final race, Le Breton turned to Gates and said that as they had the pick of positions one and three, Gates should take the inside berth because it was easily the best on the track. 'I'm too tired to do anything,' said Le Breton. 'I'm so tired.'*

*Nobody knows whether Ken had done anything physically out of the ordinary that day or whether, perhaps, he was suffering from 'flu', but he was out of sorts on the track and rode well below his best. I put his fatal accident down to a simple error of judgement, possibly brought on by, as Jack Gates still remembers, his strange tiredness.*

*In hindsight, Ken's Australian performances that season were well below the standard he had achieved in the previous British summer campaign.*

As to the reasons, the search must go a little deeper. Perhaps it was indeed that simple, he was over-tired. For almost ten years he had been on the go, forever on the move, his military career had been extremely arduous, and in his speedway days there were times when he seldom slept in the same place twice. It is hard to imagine today, in our hi-tech modern style of living, with easy movement and conveniences, how painstakingly slow and difficult life was in the late 1940s. There may have been odd signs of wavering now and then, to judge from his results and scores, but a young man in the prime of life would have just shrugged off such omens.

He obviously must have had some inner worries about maintaining a level of consistency, but this again would be nothing new to him, just another test of courage and endurance. He would dig deep and rally himself as always. He was obviously into the far reaches of his mental and physical exhaustion by the time of his death, that much was apparent. Simply put, he was past the point of no return. For the first time in his life he was confronting his pace of continual maximum effort, but was possibly unable to comprehend an outcome for this level of exertion.

There is no means of determining what exactly a maximum effort is – there is no scale, no record, no tangible graph upon which to determine a cut-off point, nothing written down to provide guidance as to when that point is reached. It is solely the province of the individual himself, he alone has that inner instinct or forewarning, however that is determined, at which juncture the mind and body says that is it, this far and no further.

All riders accept the fact that speedway is dangerous, that there will be accidents as well as fatalities. A list of the possible reasons/causes for Le Breton's death on that evening presents itself for debate:

a) Mentally and physically depressed (post-traumatic stress disorder).

b) Physical exhaustion.

c) Rumours persist that he slipped/fell in or out of the bath/shower banging his head, which left him with a headache, nausea, physically sick.

d) A viral infection/stomach bug/diarrhoea/high temperature/fever or flu/gastro-enteritis.

e) Pressuring himself to regain his rising standard/wrong mechanical set-up/timings/wrong gear/engine problems etc.

f) Daily harassment about his future/contracts/transfer/financial matters etc.

g) The ever-increasing publicity glare and lack of privacy.

h) Family ultimatums, wife/family wanting him to retire.

i) Outside business offers.

j) Family illness/bereavement.

k) Premonition, psychic intuition.

l) Track conditions.

m) A feud.

n) Riders did not receive a medical before a meeting. There is reason to suspect therefore that if he had had to have a medical before the race then the doctor would have declared him unfit to race.

It is a well-known fact that servicemen who fought in jungle campaigns were given Mepacrine to suppress the effects of malaria. Tropical hygiene itself is a subject that would fill a book. If a reason must be sought for Ken's passing, then in all probability it lies here. Malaria is treatable, but it can only be held at bay. Once the sufferer is away from tropical conditions, however, its effects become less with the passage of time. The virus remains within the body, and every so often the victim is liable to experience a bout of high fever, sweating, cold spasms and shivering, accompanied by nagging thumping headaches, on and off for perhaps two or three days. These symptoms reduce the victim to a state of lethargy. Drinking gallons of water helps, but the sight of food is sickening. Much like a migraine headache, noise and bright lights only add further problems (anyone who has ever been to a speedway meeting knows the amount of sonic vibrations that can emanate, especially in a confined pits area). He may have had a slight malarial reoccurrence that particular night, this would certainly account for his apparent tiredness. Nobody but himself would have been able to detect this condition.

When a rider is killed there is great sadness, particularly if he was a close friend and was well liked. It is said that time hardens one's feelings and the soul becomes inured when some friend is taken from us, and that no tragedy will hit so hard ever afterwards. This may be true. A death, however, means an absence, a wiping of the slate, if not the memory. Speedway has taken the lives of many a good man, but always, except for those outside the rider's immediate family, there is the convenient and consoling thought that 'the guy knew what he was doing and knew the risks, nobody made him do it'. Accidents tend to be all or nothing. A man dies, or recovers, even if he is maimed and crippled for life, which is even harder to accept. Any normal person will feel sadness, so when something like that happens you feel desperation, and ashamed. It is a world that few people even care to think about; they just simply prefer to ignore it. Even so, the loss is extremely hard to bear for all concerned.

Speedway riders are ordinary people, it is just that they are involved in an extraordinary endeavour, and unless an individual has, being blunt, put his life and limb in mortal danger, who are they to question the reasoning. Le Breton, one suspects, had a healthy respect for death, but I do honestly believe he had no fear of it. He had been brought up in a religious family, and his faith had already been severely tested in a war situation. He would have lost some close friends in New Guinea, and no person should be made to face that kind of horror, far less endure it. God is the only one who can say this far and no further. He chooses the moment, and it matters not where you are: crossing the street, in church, or up to your neck in some filthy swamp in the back of beyond, watching your friends die around you. It can happen anywhere, even on a speedway track! Le Breton would have clung to this philosophy. As Ken once said:

*One of my relations was active all his life, laboured at many jobs, fought in wars, had been shipwrecked, trekked across the continent, and he died in bed, ninety-nine years old. It was just his time.*

Destiny, Fate, Chance, call it what you will. The fact remains he was burnt out. The flame could not be rekindled. This biography offers glimpses of his loyalty to others and the unfailing generosity of his nature. If, at the end, Ken perished because of that loyalty and that generosity, it was at least fitting. Precisely why that is so may now be more apparent, in discovering what he achieved and what he may have gone on to garner. For it is there, and there alone, that we discern the lasting validity of his life and work.

# Ten

# TRIBUTES AND SOLILOQUY

The tributes listed below are only a small selection picked at random.

Ken was larger than life. His riding was visually dramatic, and the image even more dramatic, He was such a charismatic figure that made people conscious of speedway. It's almost difficult to talk about him.

*Roy Bishop*

When you rode against Ken or with him, you had to raise your level to his. HE insisted upon that.

*Jack Young*

Just about anything but speedway was superfluous for Ken. He was the most intensely involved rider of speedway you may care to name. Nobody can ever remember him asking about cricket or a good place to eat. All he thought about was how the team would perform on the night.

*Graham Warren*

A great guy, and a very nice man. You couldn't help but like him. He was just that kind of a person. We had some fine scraps. Whenever speedway gets talked about, sooner or later, his name comes up.

*Jack Parker*

We all need heroes. Ken was mine. I always wanted to have a style like that, so did everybody else. That, I do believe is consistent with good taste, and I have always been associated with those who have good taste. Ken never went too far out of his way for anything good or bad. I do honestly think if he had just been a bit more patient, what was right for him would surely have come along before much longer. He loved everybody and hated nobody, he had a good solid background, so he never really felt insecure like so many others, that is a nice feeling for anyone. He wasn't complex like most people you meet, trying to share his well-being with everyone. Many thought him rather strange, but there was a glow, hard to explain, but you felt happy inside your-self whenever he was around. I'll say this, when a chap like him goes, there is not many who can take his place. It is easy to miss him now.

*Jack Winstanley*

I feel Ken went the way he wished, and he fulfilled his mission in life.

*Vic Duggan*

He was my idol. I got to talk to him a lot. I think he liked me. He would find time to pass on tips. It was simply great that he would keep an eye on me. Every so often, he would tell me, ' you've got it, keep it going, you've got it now '. He didn't have to, but he did. There wasn't many guys that offered to help in those days, it was such a cut-throat business. You would see him whispering in someone's ear and giving them a little pat on the back. That was the kind of guy he was.

*Fred Rogers*

I had just recently come out of the Forces and was getting started. Ken's stature at that time, led me to think he was unapproachable. Sort of aloof, but that was far from it. Being ex-servicemen, we got on pretty well. He was very interested in my experiences. We often joked about army life. Without ever asking, whenever we met, he always enquired how I was getting on, and offered advice and practical solutions to whatever technical problems I was having. It was never a problem for him; he was just that kind of a guy. He really was all the things people say about him. A genuine, warm, kind, friendly guy, very intelligent. It was an immense delight to be in his company, he radi-ated a presence that you couldn't help but like. Today, people would sneer at you for saying something like that, but you know, every so often, someone enters your life to such an extent that you can never forget them. I guess he is greatly missed by many fellows like me. I suppose he has a place in all our hearts, I know he has in mine.

*Gordon McGregor*

A warm and decent man. There's not many can be called that. The kind of exposure he gave to speedway has never been fully recognised, but that he was able to, says a lot. For those of us who were part of it, he left us all a legacy by which we are all remembered today.

*Dick Campbell*

You never heard a bad word about him. A likeable guy. Especially when you consider what a rat-race speedway is. He once told me, the hardest thing in life is living with success. It couldn't have been easy for him. There were moments of tragedy that marked his life. The losses are often greater than the gains, they tell you. Ken gained the greatest of possessions... equanimity.

*Merv Harding*

Ken. Where do you begin? I would like to think I was his friend. He had many acquaintances that I do know, but friends? I don't think he allowed many people to get close to him, But, he was one of the nicest guys that ever lived.

*Ken McKinlay*

Like the best of them, he was able to concentrate on his riding. He had this ability in him to switch on to do what he had to do. It was uncanny.

*Keith Gurtner*

He told me once, 'training schools are very fine, but practise and develop your own ideas. I'll tell you this,' he said, 'first, find the logical way, then when you've got it, avoid it like the devil, and let your inner self guide you, and don't be like anyone else.'

*Noel Watson*

Admired by his opponents, for the many targets he set them. By the fans for the artistry he left them. Like all the great Australian riders before him, he had that kind of smooth style that people like – flowing, immaculate – the hardest part, I suppose, was to make it look good. So easy did he make it, everybody thought they could do the same. Therein, lies the art of the man.

*Frank Varey*

Ken and Joan were very close. He would watch over her, always at her side, whenever she might need help, a word of prayer, or someone to call the doctor. You know, whenever I had some problems, I would pay them a visit, we would have a meal. They would provide me with a few words of encouragement. Being in their presence was humbling, they never said much, but there was a special loving feeling that surrounded them, and it enveloped whoever came into contact with them. I would leave feeling much better than when I arrived. My mother used to say, not to worry, there is always someone on hand to help point the way for me to go. They will be there when you need it the most. Joan and Ken were there. You don't forget things like that easily.

They would go any length to support me. They were always there as a witness, to be leaned on in any of my weakened positions, to defend me, to provide encouragement, but they would not hesitate in disagreeing with me when I might have said or done something that was not right for me. They were there to stop me from doing something that might harm me, or someone we all liked or loved, or considered too precious to be without protection. They both had something intangible as friends. They were both very rare species of human beings. Joan had a dignity that demanded respect, such a delicate beauty that belied her great strength of character. They were made for each other. They helped me when I needed it the most. I only wish I could have told them. We were at opposite ends of life, you know, but it mattered little to him. He reached out and made me welcome, at a time when most people avoided me for a variety of reasons. I really liked the man. I did not like the way he got treated to put it mildly! So I kinda looked out for him. He wanted me to go out to Australia with them, I wish I had. There he was… gone.

*Bruce Semmens*

Nobody dies in this world… all of us create an aura that carries on long afterwards.

*Aub Lawson*

Ken never said an ill word about anyone, that much, I do recall. He had a simple philosophy, do good get good, do bad get bad. He was a fanatic about speedway, knew it inside and out. He loved the life, but I think he saw it as a means to an end. He reached the top and stayed there, it was what he wanted, and that was the way it was.

*Johnny Duffy*

People don't believe me. Ken Le Breton was a nice guy, mind you, I've seen them come and go over the years. Those who were fortunate to have seen him, knew, that he was going to be the best ever. He is missed by all of us, for his company, and good loving care and thoughtfulness.

*Norrie Isbister*

He could have the shirt off my back any day. He left behind an echo; I still feel it to this very day.

*Tommy Miller*

Ken passed away without regaining consciousness, in St Vincent's Hospital, Sydney. The cause of death was severe head injuries, a fractured skull and a punctured lung. His mother, Mary, was at his bedside when he died. This must have been absolutely devastating for her, to lose all her sons. The family were understandingly very distraught in their grief.

Tuesday 9 January 1951 was a simply beautiful day and the sun shone brightly. The funeral was held at Sydney's Woronora Crematorium. A stunned and reverent circle of fellow riders, family and friends paid farewell that summer's day to a man who loved his fans as much as he had his speedway — with a passion that has far outlived the man himself. Among the pallbearers were riders from both the Australian and England Test teams. There were over 1,000 mourners present at the service, including many representative bodies. A police escort was also provided for the cortege of some fifty-five vehicles.

His ashes were scattered by his father, Frank senior, later and privately over the graves of Ken's two brothers at Rookwood Cemetery. The sadness caused by his loss was profound. His wife, Joan, more or less became a recluse; her stated desire and request was to be left alone. The family eventually lost contact with her. When last heard of, she had moved away, remarried, and built herself a new life away from speedway altogether.

Frank senior took it quite hard, never fully getting over his son's death, and often being quite melancholy. He passed away himself after a boating accident in 1959. The Le Breton womenfolk endured much pain and tragedy in their lives. They bore their anguish with a fierce sense of pride and dignity. Ken's mother passed away peacefully in 1989, and his sister Kathleen was seventy-two when she passed away suddenly in 1998. Of the family, there is now only Marie, a very charming, sweet and lovely person.

The distinction between sight and sound is something that has been overlooked by those who seek merely to casually remember the Le Breton image. Many critics, whose comments since Ken's untimely death are clearly influenced by vague memories of how he must have looked out there on the track, also overlook it. However, it was the sound of his engine, which still somehow seems to reverberate in the corridors of people's minds, which provides a recurring echo, and is lovingly referred to as a kind of 'sweet purr'. Anyone who has ever heard or seen a Spitfire, P51 Mustang, MV. Augusta or perhaps the W196 Mercedes-Benz, will know the feel and smell of that sound. A racing JAP could produce a pure quality of sound if it was tuned to perfection by the hands of a master.

Of course, Ken played on his image at times, and perhaps some of the presentation may have been excessive, but it was his to make. While some of the criticism may have been warranted, even the claim that this was what the fans wanted is a feeble excuse. The smooth way he handled his bodily contortions and the whole-heartedness with which he threw himself into his riding was not just something he put on solely for public appearances. Those who saw him practice behind closed doors attest that he behaved in exactly the same way. Every time he rode, he committed himself totally, especially in the physical sense, to his performances.

Setting aside his visual image and its impact, and considering only his speedway record, Ken showed better than many other riders just how important were early influences. From the pioneers he took the essence of showmanship and good timekeeping, from his own humble beginnings he took the extrovert Australian characterisation and wrapped it up in a form of dynamic noisy enthusiasm, and from here in Britain he added the sophisticated showbiz elements. There was commercialism, which doubtless brought down on him the wrath of those who deplored the commercialisation of speedway in general.

This is why, in the great scheme of machinations, that Hoskins and Le Breton gravitated towards each other; like attracts like. As discussed, the heady atmosphere during the 'heyday' of pre-war speedway was inextricably linked to a period of acute economic depression; it is therefore difficult to accuse or to mount a wholly supportable critique of those within speedway for 'selling out'. It would have been impossible for any rider (especially if he had the slightest trace of sensitivity) who had, during those years, seen or known at first hand the poverty and hard times, and to also have come through a horrendous war, to try and effect a change of attitude. In Ken's case, he chose deliberately to fall back on that concept, capitalising on his resulting popularity to ensure a future for himself and his family.

Le Breton was simply a creature of his times and of his environment. In the course of his career, he became a symbol of those times through which he lived. Long after the 'heyday', the 'boom-years', the resurgence of the 1970/80s, and on to the new era of today, Ken Le Breton remains one of speedway's most enduring images. It was a combination of things that made him special, only Le Breton seemed to have more of these attributes than any other rider. There was not one single quality that made him what he had become. It was a combination of factors and circumstance, added to his fierce competitive nature and will to win, coupled to an intelligent approach to speedway in general.

There is no disputing the contribution made by Ken to speedway. It is to his credit that for all the time he was in speedway he never featured the 'White Ghost' image excessively. He was smart enough to know that the customers he attracted with his showmanship could be quickly turned off by his inordinate number of tearaway wins. The quality of his kind of racing was always so high that little else was required to sell to the average discriminating fan. Many would agree that Ken's ability to drive and lead a team was one of his greatest assets, and that he did it without being in the spotlight every minute of a meeting.

With the passing of any great sportsman, there is always a gap left. In time this gap closes to a niche, but that niche is never filled by another. So it is that Ken Le Breton's place in that niche will never be taken. Everybody's part in life is a cross that has to be borne, especially if they become well known and are good at what they do.

Ken acquired a tremendous reputation, and one of the dangers of having such a reputation is that everybody wants to have a go at it! Ken is now no longer with us to defend that reputation in the only way possible... out on the track. This was a great loss not only to those who were closest to him, his parents and family, but to his competitors, for they were never ever able to challenge that reputation. It has remained unsullied to this very day.

Speedway had, in Ken Le Breton, a superb ambassador; he was a proud and very polite Australian. He demanded little, but rewarded those who were loyal to him, who believed and had faith in him, with a friendship that was very personal and special. He will be long remembered by all those who had the pleasure of that friendship, and of representing speedway as it ought to have been seen by outsiders. In time, he would have added yet more lustre to its cause. He always raced so brilliantly; it was so easy to imagine that nothing would ever happen to him. Unfortunately, we also forget the part that luck plays in our lives. Ken Le Breton didn't run out of skill, he simply ran out of luck.

After the funeral, the family entertained his close friends; it turned out to be a very happy affair, much more than anyone ever imagined. Ken would have liked that. It was a sincere tribute to him.

So, who was he, really? A man of simplicity and an irrepressible spirit. His beliefs were few, clear and uncomplicated. He approached tasks, issues and relationships with uncommon directness. He seldom disassembled. Although utterly practical, he was also very emotional, a sentimentalist. He was deeply moved by the love of animals. In everyday dealings with people little deterred him, although his articulation of his innermost deeper feelings were harder to reveal.

Very much a product of his times, he divided people into classes, often pre-judging them accordingly, and was invariably content with his own assumptions. This was the way he had been brought up — it didn't preclude him from broadening his horizons and opinions as he saw fit, however. He was intelligent and quick-witted, yet in spite of an endless source of ready-made ideas he was not overtly analytical. He needed the time to work ideas through. In his personal life, he was perhaps a victim, having had to rely upon his own resources from an early age. Inclined towards loneliness, his real emotions carefully guarded by a carapace of stubbornness.

His personality was a mixture of reflexive emotions, full of contradictions, veering between modesty and egotism, sensitivity and boorishness, joy and happiness, sometimes on odd occasions taking his cue from those closest to him. In the company of seniors, he could be unpretentious, even diffident. His equals saw his open-handed, lively candour. Those he considered beneath his stature might catch his casual offhandedness, sometimes a careless cruelty, but it had no meaning behind it. Everything he did was full of boundless energy. He was an accomplished rider more than a great rider. Those he raced against may have had better skills, but few could match his single-minded determination to succeed in whatever he chose to do. As a leader, his determination, will and ability to drive others to do likewise was his hallmark. He was versatile enough, aided by a sharp eye and a keen ear, to engage fully with whatever task was in hand, be it racing, mechanical, making speeches, writing, his charity work, etc. Perhaps, because of having this kind of nature, he may have stretched his limits.

Those who loved and liked him did so, intently. Others regarded him with a wary respect, some thought him rebarbative. A few found him insufferable. A strange loneliness seemed to shadow him; it may well be that his wife, Joan, managed to assuage his inner isolation, for he was most definitely happy in her company. It could be argued that he ought to have eased up, settling for what he had already achieved, and maybe those who he looked towards might have insisted a little more that this was what he should do.

Johnnie Hoskins once described Ken 'As great a rider as the sport of speedway has ever known.' Perhaps he was right, for Le Breton had served him well. Be that as it may, the main focus in his life was speedway, all else was subordinate to it. He sought nothing less than perfection. Beyond his innate talent there was constant study and application, and ceaseless practising; he had the discipline of a martinet for himself and for those close to him, to ensure his determination to reach the pinnacle. In that he succeeded.

History will judge him on what he accomplished. What we long for, we can usually never quite obtain, and yet we keep on reaching for it. Even though we have no reason to be sure of the outcome, we cling to our faith that the effort will not go un-rewarded. Ken Le Breton had this knowing trust in the process of life. A willingness to hope for the best, even when it was unrealistic to expect it.

For many, Ken was simply a hero they would see no more, a man who briefly enriched their lives. He had combined and cultivated the art of racing to the highest point of perfection, with a true sense of absolute fairness. No half measures, just plain enthusiasm. As an individual, he was ever the charming, good-natured fellow, and few could really find fault with him. He was entirely without guile, he said what he felt, without fear or favour, whether or not it might profit or injure him. He will remain in our hearts and minds as a good friend, a fair sportsman, and a kind and decent human being.

We are thankful for Ken Le Breton and may 'God Bless Him' and minimise the grief of his family and relatives, who may be assured of the great love felt for him by all of us, his friends.

It was Johnnie Hoskins' wish for this soliloquy to be included:

*Ken Le Breton, a gentler person never lived, a man with the greatest of courage, the most majestic stature, highly skilled in many virtues, a man of impeccable taste who commanded the respect and admiration of many people. His fans at home and abroad marvelled at the grandeur of his talent and the mantle of his supremacy that he wore with grace. He was adored by a wide range of friends, poor, rich, the famous and unknowns. We all pay homage to Ken's God-given ability and mastery of his craft. Because he had a rare sensitivity and applied himself to his gifts, Ken was successful in blending them into an unforgettable dream that none will ever forget. Skill, charm, call it what you will, he gave nothing but happiness to all who came into contact with him. His greatest virtue was his honesty, not only to others, but also to himself. He demanded freedom of expression. He was totally intolerant when or if a compromise was expected or considered expedient. He lived in what we consider the most important and moral of freedoms... freedom of hate, freedom of self-pity (even throughout the pain and bad news). Freedom from fear of possibly doing something that might help another more than it might himself, and freedom from the kind of pride that could make a man feel that he was better than his brother or neighbour. His patience was incomparable and unlimited. He had no aspirations other than to be the best of what he could be. Yet the legacy he leaves, will never be less than the ultimate on the highest plateau whether by compassion or not. Let us therefore not mourn too much for Ken; he has, in truth, only stepped through a door, through which, whenever we choose, [we] may catch a glimpse of his image, still smiling happily. He shared his life with us; so let us share the memory he gave us.*

# SUMMARY OF TEAMS' STATISTICS
# AND RESULTS 1947–1950

This section provides an in-depth analysis of all the fixtures that Ken was known to have competed in (either with his current team or on an individual basis) during his racing career, whilst here in Britain. Every effort has been taken to ensure that the details here are as correct as far as is known, but in such a work as this there may well be errors of one sort or another. It has been divided into five parts, each of which covers a specific year. Also included are those Test Series fixtures, both official and unofficial, that Ken participated in, and these are incorporated into the calendar date sequence.

The results begin with Ken's introduction as a member of the New Cross Rangers, on 30 April 1947, right through until his last meeting on 10 October 1950 for the Ashfield Giants.

The abbreviations used, are as follows:

| | |
|---|---|
| INT. CH | International Challenge Matches |
| INT. TEST | International Matches |
| NL1 | National League, Division One |
| NL2 | National League, Division Two |
| BSC | British Speedway Cup Match |
| AC | Anniversary Cup Match |
| NT | National Trophy Cup Match – Second Division Section |
| CH | Challenge Match |
| NS | Northern Section of Kemsley Shield |
| IND. | Individual Meeting |
| WCQR | World Championship Qualifying Round |
| BRCQR | British Riders Championship Qualifying Round |
| SRC | Scottish Riders Championship |
| agg. | Aggregate score |
| (dnr) | Did Not Ride |
| (r) | Reserve |

Please note that unless stated, all time measurements are in seconds.

Due to restrictions, a commercial decision was taken to not to include a complete itemised listing of heat details etc. for all the meetings indicated. In order to present a final plenary, statistic-wise, all the matches which Ken did not compete in (although he was still part of that team) are also included.

**1947 SEASON**

*1) New Cross Rangers*

League Points scored by New Cross riders for the 1947 season:

| | | | |
|---|---|---|---|
| Ron Johnson | 194 | Frank Lawrence | 38 |
| Bill Longley | 185 | Mick Mitchell | 35 |
| Geoff Pymar | 163 | Keith Harvey | 5 |
| Eric French | 122 | George Gower | 2 |
| Jeff Lloyd | 93 | **Ken Le Breton** | 2 |
| Lionel Van Praag | 89 | Don Hardy | 1 |
| Ray Moore | 66 | | |

National League Division One:

| Team | PL | W | D | L | Pts |
|---|---|---|---|---|---|
| Wembley | 24 | 19 | 0 | 5 | 38 |
| Belle Vue | 24 | 15 | 1 | 8 | 31 |
| Wimbledon | 24 | 13 | 1 | 10 | 27 |
| Odsal | 24 | 10 | 1 | 13 | 21 |
| **New Cross** | 24 | 10 | 0 | 14 | 20 |
| West Ham | 24 | 8 | 0 | 16 | 16 |
| Harringay | 24 | 7 | 1 | 16 | 15 |

*2) Newcastle Diamonds*

League and Cup points scored by Newcastle riders in 1947:

| | | | |
|---|---|---|---|
| Wilf Jay | 437.5 | Bonny Waddell | 79 |
| Norman Evans | 423.5 | Danny Calder | 25 |
| Doug McLachlan | 406 | Pat Smith | 20 |
| Alec Grant | 282.5 | Harry Modral | 6 |
| Jack Hunt | 120.5 | Stan Pennell | 4 |
| **Ken Le Breton** | 120 | Phil Day | 3 |
| Jeff Lloyd | 98.5 | Ray Muir | 2 |
| Peter Lloyd | 88 | | |

British Speedway Cup Division Two:

| Team | PL | W | D | L | Pts |
|------|----|----|----|----|-----|
| Sheffield | 14 | 11 | 0 | 3 | 26 |
| Middlesbrough | 14 | 9 | 0 | 5 | 21 |
| Norwich | 14 | 7 | 0 | 7 | 14 |
| **Newcastle** | **14** | **7** | **0** | **7** | **14** |
| Wigan | 14 | 6 | 0 | 8 | 12 |
| Bristol | 14 | 6 | 0 | 8 | 12 |
| Glasgow | 14 | 5 | 0 | 9 | 10 |
| Birmingham | 14 | 5 | 0 | 9 | 10 |

*(3 points were awarded for an away win in the British Speedway Cup.)*

National League Division Two:

| Team | PL | W | D | L | Pts |
|------|----|----|----|----|-----|
| Middlesbrough | 28 | 20 | 0 | 8 | 40 |
| Sheffield | 28 | 17 | 2 | 9 | 36 |
| Norwich | 28 | 16 | 0 | 12 | 32 |
| Birmingham | 28 | 14 | 0 | 14 | 28 |
| **Newcastle** | **28** | **12** | **2** | **14** | **26** |
| Bristol | 28 | 11 | 0 | 17 | 22 |
| Wigan | 28 | 9 | 2 | 17 | 20 |
| Glasgow | 28 | 10 | 0 | 18 | 20 |

## 1948 SEASON

### 3) Newcastle Diamonds

League and Cup points scored by Newcastle riders in 1948:

| | | | |
|---|---|---|---|
| Wilf Jay | 363 | Billy Bales | 12 |
| Norman Evans | 317 | *(borrowed from Yarmouth)* | |
| Alec Grant | 285 | Alan Hunt | 5 |
| **Ken Le Breton** | **273** | *(borrowed from Cradley Heath)* | |
| Charlie Spinks | 162 | Jack Winstanley | 4 |
| Jack Hunt | 160 | Bonny Waddell | 4 |
| Danny Calder | 98 | Jack Martin | 2 |
| Keith Gurtner | 83 | Fred Brand | 0 |
| Maurice Stobbart | 80 | *(borrowed from Yarmouth)* | |
| E.D. Pye | 67 | Ray Muir | 0 |
| Peter Lloyd | 54 | A. Gardner | 0 |
| Rol Stobbart | 31 | *(borrowed from Bristol?)* | |
| Fred Rogers | 28 | ? Talbot | 0 |
| Derek Close | 14 | *(borrowed from Yarmouth?)* | |

Anniversary Cup Division Two:

| Team | PL | W | D | L | Pts |
|------|-----|----|----|----|-----|
| Birmingham | 16 | 12 | 0 | 4 | 29 |
| Sheffield | 16 | 9 | 0 | 7 | 19 |
| Glasgow | 16 | 8 | 0 | 8 | 17 |
| Middlesbrough | 16 | 8 | 0 | 8 | 17 |
| Norwich | 16 | 7 | 1 | 8 | 16 |
| Fleetwood | 16 | 7 | 1 | 8 | 16 |
| Bristol | 16 | 8 | 0 | 8 | 16 |
| **Newcastle** | **16** | **6** | **0** | **10** | **12** |
| Edinburgh | 16 | 6 | 0 | 10 | 12 |

*(3 points were awarded for an away win, and 2 points for an away draw.)*

National League Division Two:

| Team | PL | W | D | L | Pts |
|------|-----|----|----|----|-----|
| Bristol | 32 | 23 | 0 | 9 | 46 |
| Birmingham | 32 | 20 | 1 | 11 | 41 |
| Middlesbrough | 32 | 18 | 2 | 12 | 38 |
| Sheffield | 32 | 17 | 1 | 14 | 35 |
| Norwich | 32 | 17 | 0 | 15 | 34 |
| Glasgow | 32 | 14 | 3 | 15 | 31 |
| **Newcastle** | **32** | **11** | **0** | **21** | **22** |
| Fleetwood | 32 | 10 | 1 | 21 | 21 |
| Edinburgh | 32 | 10 | 0 | 22 | 20 |

**1949** SEASON

*4) Ashfield Giants*

League and Cup points scored by Ashfield riders in 1949:

| | | | |
|---|---|---|---|
| **Ken Le Breton** | **414** | Jim Reid | 5 |
| Merv Harding | 373 | Johnny Bradford | 3 |
| Keith Gurtner | 280 | *(borrowed from Plymouth)* | |
| Alec Grant | 183 | Peter Lloyd | 2 |
| Norman Evans | 127 | Jack Martin | 2 |
| Willie Wilson | 113 | Bert Croucher | 2 |
| Gruff Garland | 100 | *(borrowed from Oxford)* | |
| Rol Stobbart | 48 | Jack Watts | 2 |
| Eric Liddell | 35 | Ron Brereton | 0 |
| Norman Johnson | 31 | *(borrowed from Newcastle)* | |
| Larry Lazarus | 9 | Maurice Stobbart | 0 |
| Johnny Davies | 6 | Fred Yates | 0 |
| *(borrowed from Norwich)* | | | |

National League Division Two:

| Team | PL | W | D | L | Pts |
|------|-----|-----|-----|-----|-----|
| Bristol | 44 | 34 | 1 | 9 | 69 |
| Sheffield | 44 | 29 | 1 | 14 | 59 |
| Norwich | 44 | 27 | 0 | 17 | 54 |
| Cradley Heath | 44 | 25 | 0 | 19 | 50 |
| Edinburgh | 44 | 24 | 0 | 20 | 48 |
| Walthamstow | 44 | 21 | 3 | 20 | 45 |
| Southampton | 44 | 21 | 3 | 20 | 45 |
| Glasgow W.C. | 44 | 20 | 0 | 24 | 40 |
| Fleetwood | 44 | 18 | 1 | 25 | 37 |
| Newcastle | 44 | 17 | 1 | 26 | 35 |
| **Ashfield** | **44** | **12** | **1** | **31** | **25** |
| Coventry | 44 | 10 | 1 | 33 | 21 |

Australia beat England 3–2 in the Test match series

## 1950 SEASON

*5) Ashfield Giants*

League and Cup points scored by Ashfield riders in 1950:

| | | | |
|------|-----|------|-----|
| **Ken Le Breton** | 508 | Norman Johnson | 17 |
| Merv Harding | 451 | Ed Noakes | 16 |
| Keith Gurtner | 294 | Geoff Godwin | 10 |
| Willie Wilson | 290 | Tom Turnham | 4 |
| Bruce Semmens | 210 | Brian Gorman | 1 |
| Bob Lovell | 161 | *(borrowed from Sheffield)* | |
| Alec Grant | 64 | Ray Harker | 0 |
| Eric Liddell | 62 | Fred Rowe | 0 |
| Bill Baird | 47 | *(borrowed from Sheffield)* | |
| Larry Lazarus | 31 | Rusty Wainwright | 0 |
| Ron Hart | 20 | | |

Kemsley Cup (Northern Section):

| Team | PL | W | D | L | Pts |
|------|-----|-----|-----|-----|-----|
| Halifax | 14 | 10 | 0 | 4 | 20 |
| **Ashfield** | **14** | **9** | **0** | **5** | **18** |
| Hanley | 14 | 8 | 1 | 5 | 17 |
| Edinburgh | 14 | 8 | 1 | 5 | 17 |
| Sheffield | 14 | 6 | 0 | 8 | 12 |
| Newcastle | 14 | 6 | 0 | 8 | 12 |
| Glasgow | 14 | 4 | 0 | 10 | 8 |
| Fleetwood | 14 | 4 | 0 | 10 | 8 |

National League Division Two:

| Team | PL | W | D | L | Pts |
|------|----|----|----|----|-----|
| Norwich | 28 | 18 | 1 | 9 | 37 |
| Glasgow | 28 | 18 | 0 | 10 | 36 |
| Cradley Heath | 28 | 18 | 0 | 10 | 36 |
| Coventry | 28 | 16 | 0 | 12 | 32 |
| Walthamstow | 28 | 16 | 0 | 12 | 32 |
| Halifax | 28 | 16 | 0 | 12 | 32 |
| Southampton | 28 | 14 | 1 | 13 | 29 |
| Edinburgh | 28 | 14 | 1 | 13 | 29 |
| Plymouth | 28 | 13 | 0 | 15 | 26 |
| Sheffield | 28 | 13 | 0 | 15 | 26 |
| **Ashfield** | **28** | **12** | **0** | **16** | **24** |
| Yarmouth | 28 | 12 | 0 | 16 | 24 |
| Newcastle | 28 | 10 | 0 | 18 | 20 |
| Hanley | 28 | 9 | 2 | 17 | 20 |
| Fleetwood | 28 | 8 | 1 | 19 | 17 |

Test series results: England beat Australia 3-2 / Overseas beat Britain 3-2

# KEN LE BRETON'S OFFICIAL MATCH RACES
## All known Invitation/Challenge Match Races/Second Half appearances

### Official Match Races: 1949

*11 May at Glasgow White City:*    Scottish Match Race Challenge Cup, 1st Leg:
                                   v Junior Bainbridge (Glasgow Tigers): Won 2-1
*23 May at Glasgow Ashfield:*      Scottish Match Race Challenge Cup, 2nd Leg:
                                   v Junior Bainbridge: Won 2-0
*14 June at Glasgow Ashfield:*     Scottish Match Race Challenge Cup, 1st Leg:
                                   v Jack Young (Edinburgh Monarchs): Won 2-0
*25 June at Edinburgh:*            Scottish Match Race Challenge Cup, 2nd Leg:
                                   v Jack Young: Lost 2-1
*27 July at Glasgow White City:*   Scottish Match Race Challenge Cup, Decider:
                                   v Jack Young: Lost 2-1
*23 August at Glasgow Ashfield:*   2nd Division Match Race Championship, 1st Leg:
                                   v Billy Hole (Bristol Bulldogs): Lost 2-0
*26 August at Bristol:*            2nd Division Match Race Championship, 2nd Leg:
                                   v Billy Hole: Lost 2-0

### Official Match Races: 1950

*2 May at Glasgow Ashfield:*       Northern Match Race Championship, 1st Leg:
                                   v Jack Young (Edinburgh Monarchs): Won 2-0
*22 May at Edinburgh:*             Northern Match Race Championship, 2nd Leg:
                                   v Jack Young: Lost 2-0
*7 June at Glasgow White City:*    Northern Match Race Championship, Decider:
                                   v Jack Young: Won 2-1
*19 June at Cradley Heath:*        2nd Division Match Race Championship, 1st Leg:
                                   v Alan Hunt (Cradley Heath Heathens): Lost 2-0
*20 June at Glasgow Ashfield:*     2nd Division Match Race Championship, 2nd Leg:
                                   v Alan Hunt: Won 2-0
*30 June at Sheffield:*            2nd Division Match Race Championship, Decider:
                                   v Alan Hunt: Won 2-1
*18 July at Glasgow Ashfield:*     2nd Division Match Race Championship, 1st Leg:
                                   v Arthur Forrest (Halifax Dukes): Won 2-0
*21 July at Halifax:*              2nd Division Match Race Championship, 2nd Leg:
                                   v Arthur Forrest:

(Note: This was postponed as Ken was injured.)

*4 August at Halifax:* 2nd Division Match Race Championship, 2nd Leg: v Arthur Forrest: Won 2–1

*17 August at Plymouth:* 2nd Division Match Race Championship, 1st Leg: v Peter Robinson (Plymouth Devils): Lost 2–1

*29 August at Glasgow Ashfield:* 2nd Division Match Race Championship, 2nd Leg: v Peter Robinson: Won 2–0

*4 September at Cradley Heath:* 2nd Division Match Race Championship, Decider: v Peter Robinson: Declared null and void. (Note: Ken missed his train from Glasgow, and was unable to appear. By the rules of the competition, the title should have gone to the opponent by forfeit but Robinson was very reluctant to have won the tie by default, insisting that a re-arranged deciding leg be made. This was agreed to.)

*15 September at Southampton:* 2nd Division Match Race Championship, re-arranged Decider: v Peter Robinson: Won 2–0

*19 September at Glasgow Ashfield:* Scottish Match Race Challenge Cup, 1st Leg: v Tommy Miller (Glasgow Tigers): Won 2–0

*20 September at Glasgow White City:* Scottish Match Race Challenge Cup, 2nd Leg: v Tommy Miller: Won 2–0

## Invitation/Challenge Match Races/Second Half Appearances: 1947

*8 September — Newcastle: Challenge Match Race* (1 race only)
  v Joe Crowther *(Glasgow)*
  1st Joe Crowther, 2nd Ken Le Breton

*21 June — Odsal (Bradford): Flaming June Scratch Races*
  1st — Fred Tuck *(Bristol)*
  2nd — Bat Byrnes *(Glasgow)*
  3rd — Archie Windmill *(Wimbledon)*
  4th — Ken Le Breton

*Cartwright Hall Scratch Races*
  1st — Dick Harris *(Wimbledon)*
  2nd — Ernie Price *(Odsal)*
  3rd — Fred Tuck *(Bristol)*
  4th — Ken Le Breton

*10 September — Glasgow White City: Challenge Match Race*
  v Buck Ryan *(Glasgow)*: Ken won 2–1
  1st leg — 1st Ken Le Breton, 2nd Buck Ryan — time 86.0
  2nd leg — 1st Buck Ryan, 2nd Ken Le Breton — time 86.2
  Deciding leg — 1st Ken Le Breton, 2nd Buck Ryan — time 92.4

*Ken also competed in the second half event, failing to reach the final.*

*Kelburn Cup Qualifying Heat* — time 88.2
  1st — Will Lowther *(Glasgow)*
  2nd — Bat Byrnes *(Glasgow)*
  3rd — Paddy Hammond *(Norwich)*
  4th — Ken Le Breton

**1948**

In spite of exhaustive research, I am unable to confirm or deny details of any Match Races or other Second Halves that Ken may have possibly participated in during the 1948 season. It could well be that he was deliberately keeping a low profile on account of the 'Swagman' film and restricted himself only to team commitments.

**1949**

*11 May – Glasgow White City*
Ken competed in the second half, won
  Qualifier and Final. *(Details unknown)*
*13 June – Newcastle*
Ken competed in the second half of the
  Newcastle / Norwich match. He rode
  in four races in about 15 minutes!
*Glasgow Scratch Race – time 75.6*
  1st – Ken Le Breton
  2nd – Jack Hodgson *(Newcastle)*
  3rd – Fred Rogers *(Norwich)*
  4th – Syd Littlewood *(Norwich)*
*Edinburgh Scratch Race: Re-Run result –* time
  75.8
  1st – Ernie Brecknell *(Newcastle)*
  2nd – Ken Le Breton
  3rd – Frank Hodgson *(Newcastle)*
  4th – Bert Spencer *(Norwich)* (excluded)
*Dundee Scratch Race – time 75.6*
  1st – Phil Clarke *(Norwich)*
  2nd – Benny King *(Newcastle)*
  3rd – Son Mitchell *(Newcastle)*
  4th – Ken Le Breton (failed to finish –
  engine failure)
*Newcastle Scratch Race – time 76.4*
  1st – Jack Hodgson *(Newcastle)*
  2nd – Frank Hodgson *(Newcastle)*
  3rd – Ernie Brecknell *(Newcastle)*
  4th – Ken Le Breton (fell)
*14 July – Wembley*
Ken competed in two Stadium Scratch
  Races in the second half
*1st race (Qualifier) – time 59.0*
  1st – Ken Le Breton
  2nd – Bob Wells *(Wembley)*
  3rd – Dick Harris *(Wimbledon)*

  4th – Jimmy Gibb *(Wimbledon)*
*2nd race (Final) – time 58.2*
  1st – Alf Bottoms *(Wembley)*
  2nd – Ken Le Breton
  3rd – Bob Wells *(Wembley)*
  4th – Bruce Abernethy *(Wembley)*
*2 August – Glasgow Ashfield*
Jet rocket-assisted bike demonstration
  held during second half, by Ken and
  Merv Harding
  1-lap clutch start: Merv Harding 15.8,
  Ken Le Breton 17.8
*4 August – Wembley*
*1-lap jet-assisted record attempt – time*
  19.2
*v Tommy Price (Wembley)*
  1st Ken Le Breton, 2nd Tommy Price.
  *Ken featured in the second half as well.*
*All Star Visitors Scratch Race*
  1st – Louis Lawson *(Belle Vue)*
  2nd – Geoff Pymar *(Harringay)*
  3rd – Norman Parker *(Wimbledon)*
  4th – Ken Le Breton
*26 August – Bristol: Senior Scratch Race –*
  time 65.8
  1st – Ken Le Breton
  2nd – Eric Salmon *(Bristol)*
  3rd – Tom Oakley *(Southampton)*
  4th – Cecil Bailey *(Southampton)*
*Final – time 64.6*
  1st – Ken Le Breton
  2nd – Billy Hole *(Bristol)*
  3rd – Roger Wise *(Bristol)*
  4th – Jimmy Squib *(Southampton)*
*14 September – Glasgow White City: Inter*
  *City Challenge Match race* (1 race only)

v Junior Bainbridge (Glasgow Tigers)
1st Ken Le Breton, 2nd Junior
Bainbridge
*Jetaway Challenge (1 race only)*
v Junior Bainbridge
1st Junior Bainbridge, 2nd Ken Le
Breton
*Ken also took part in the second half, win-*
*ning his qualifying heat and coming 3rd in*
*the final. (Further details unknown)*
*4 October — Glasgow Ashfield: Special*
*Challenge Match Race*
v Vic Duggan *(Harringay):* Ken Le
Breton won 2-0 (times were 66.4 and
66.2)
*6 October — Glasgow Ashfield*
Ken rode in the second half as an added
attraction for the sell-out crowd.

*Vliegende Hollanders Trophy*
*Qualifying Heat* — time 72.2
1st — Ken Le Breton
2nd — Alf McIntosh *(Glasgow Tigers)*
3rd — Henk Verhouf
4th — Bert Houweling (fell)
*Final* — time 69.6
1st — Jock Grierson *(Leicester)*
2nd — Ken Le Breton
3rd — Gordon McGregor *(Glasgow*
*Tigers)*
4th — Willie Wilson *(Ashfield)*
*Extra Race* — time 69.6
1st — Ken Le Breton
2nd — Gordon McGregor *(Glasgow*
*Tigers)*
3rd — Eric Liddell *(Ashfield)*
4th — Willie Wilson *(Ashfield)*

## 1950

*26 May — Exeter: Special Challenge Match*
*Race*
v Don Hardy *(Exeter):* Ken won 2-1
*13 June — Glasgow Ashfield: Grand Challenge*
*Match Race*
v Vic Duggan *(Harringay):* Match Race
cancelled after 2nd heat
1st leg — 1st Vic Duggan, 2nd Ken Le
Breton: time — 65.4
2nd leg — Ken was awarded the race.
*(In this race, the two riders crashed heavily.*
*Duggan was badly shaken-up, and took no*
*further part)*
*15 June — Wembley: International Scratch Race*
— time 55.2
1st — Ken Le Breton
2nd — Fred Williams *(Wembley)*
3rd — George Wilks *(Wembley)*
4th — Geoff Bennett *(Birmingham)*
*1st Semi-Final* — time 56.2
1st — Ken Le Breton
2nd — Fred Williams *(Wembley)*
3rd — Eric Williams *(Wembley)*
4th — Bill Kitchen *(Wembley)*

*Final* — time 55.8
1st — Ken Le Breton
2nd — Tommy Price *(Wembley)*
3rd — Bill Gilbert *(Wembley)*
4th — Fred Williams *(Wembley)*
*29 June — Wembley: Two-Lap Dash Cup —*
*Rolling Start (Match Race) (1 race only)*
v Tommy Price *(Wembley)*
1st Ken Le Breton, 2nd Tommy Price.
*(Note: Ken set a new 2-Lap Track Record*
*— 35.2 secs = 43.93mph. The 2-Lap Track*
*Record had stood for twelve years, being set*
*by Lionel Van Praag at 36.0.) Ken also*
*competed in the second half*
*International Scratch Race* — time 56.2
1st — Bill Gilbert *(Wembley)*
2nd — Ken Le Breton
3rd — Eric Williams *(Wembley)*
4th — Oliver Hart *(Odsal)*
*Semi-final* — time 55.8
1st — Ken Le Breton
2nd — Fred Williams *(Wembley)*
3rd — Eddie Rigg *(Odsal)*
4th — Bill Gilbert *(Wembley)*

*Final* – time 56.2

1st – Ken Le Breton

2nd – George Wilks *(Wembley)*

3rd – Fred Williams *(Wembley)*

4th – Cyril Brine *(Wembley)*

*10 July – Wimbledon*

Ken may have ridden in the second half here – *(details unknown)*

*15 July – Hanley*

Ken may have ridden in the second half here – *(details unknown)*

*27 July – Wembley*

Ken was booked to appear, but due to injury cancelled

*1 August – Glasgow Ashfield*

Jet rocket-assisted bike demonstration held by Ken and Merv Harding

*5 August – Glasgow Ashfield: Inter-track Match Race* – (1 race only over 3 laps)

v Bill Carruthers *(Yarmouth)*

1st Ken Le Breton, 2nd Bill Carruthers – time 54.0

*11 August – Harringay: Special Match Race*

v Louis Lawson *(Belle Vue)*: Ken won 2–0

*8 September – Harringay*

Match Race against Split Waterman cancelled. Ken competed in second half

*International Cup*

Ken won both his qualifying heat and the final – *(details unknown)*

*23 September – Belle Vue*

Meeting postponed

*10 October – Glasgow Ashfield: World and Scottish Champions Match Race*

v Freddie Williams *(Wembley)*: Freddie Williams won 2–0 (times were 66.0 and 66.4)

# AUSTRALIAN & NEW ZEALAND
# RESULTS 1946–1951

Records for this period are not readily available. Meetings were either genuine speedway events, or a combination of solo / sidecars / midget cars etc. The majority consisted of open invitation, handicap-style racing format featuring six riders per race.

## 1946

Ken had been riding speedway for nearly six months by the time of the first recorded mention, with his now-legendary public debut at the Sydney Sports Ground on 17 May. This was the night when he may well have donned his 'famous' white leathers for the first time, and proved to be the 'sensation' of the meeting.

*17 May 1946 – (Sydney Sports Ground)*
    Ken won three races, details unknown, except 4-Lap Handicap Final – time 76.80
    1st – Aub Lawson (handicap – 130yds behind)
    2nd – Ken Le Breton (handicap – 20yds ahead)
    3rd – Norman Clay (handicap – 60yds behind)
    Hereafter Ken was handicapped to 30yds

## 1947/48

*7 November – (Sydney Sports Ground): Open Handicap Heat 5*
    1st – Cliff Watson (100yds behind)
    2nd – Don Lawson (scratch)
    3rd – Ken Le Breton (70yds behind)
*8 November – (Melbourne)*
    A series of Match Races was held reaching the final finishing behind Jack Biggs and Eric Chitty
    Ken also competed in the following:
*2-lap Handicap Race – time 46.4*
    1st – Fred Tracey
    2nd – Jack Biggs
    3rd – Ken Le Breton

*14 November – (Sydney Sports Ground): Open Handicap Qualifier*
    1st – Ken Le Breton
    2nd – Max Grosskreutz
    3rd – Jack Arnfield
    *Ken qualified for the final – (details unknown)*
*21 November – (Sydney Sports Ground)*
    Ken reached the Junior Scratch Final
    1st – Bill Melluish
    2nd – Ken Le Breton
    3rd – Norman Clay
*28 November – (Melbourne)*
    Ken reached the Handicap Final
    1st – ? Thomas

2nd – M. Pearce

3rd – Ken Le Breton

*5 December – (Sydney Sports Ground):*
  *Wimbledon Solo Handicap*
  *Qualifying Heat*
  1st – Ken Le Breton
  2nd – Bill Melluish
  3rd – Eric Chitty
  *Final*
  1st – Cliff Watson
  2nd – Ken Le Breton
  3rd – Bat Byrnes
  *Solo Scratch Race*
  1st – Jack Arnfield
  2nd – Lionel Levy
  3rd – Ken Le Breton

*20 December – (Newcastle)*
  *Frank Dolan's Team 29*
  Frank Dolan 8, Aub Lawson 7, Jack
    Arnfield 7, Ken Le Breton 3, Lionel
    Levy 2, Dick Harris 2
  *Ray Duggan's Team 25*
  Dent Oliver 7, Bill Melluish 7, Ray
    Duggan 4, Cliff Watson 3, Ernie
    Brecknell 3, Norman Clay 1
  *Solo Handicap Race*
  1st – Cliff Watson
  2nd – Lionel Levy
  3rd – Ken Le Breton

*27 December – (Newcastle)*
  *Max Grosskeutz's Team 36*
  Max Grosskreutz 9, Aub Lawson 8,
    Ernie Brecknell 8, Cliff Watson 5, Bill
    Melluish 4, Lionel Levy 1, Ken Le
    Breton (res) 1
  *Norman Parker's Team 18*
  Norman Parker 8, Dent Oliver 4, Jack
    Arnfield 2, Frank Dolan 2, Dick
    Harris 2, Norman Clay 0

*9 January 1948 – (Sydney Sports Ground):*
  *Junior Challenge Match Race (1 race – 2*
  *laps rolling start)*
  v Lionel Levy:
  1st Lionel Levy, 2nd Ken Le Breton

*Junior Scratch Race Qualifying Heat*
  1st – Ken Le Breton
  2nd – Owen Gyles
  3rd – Norman Clay
  4th – Don Lawson
  *Final*
  1st – Lionel Levy
  2nd – Hugh Geddes
  3rd – Ken Le Breton
  4th – Owen Gyles

*10 January – (Newcastle)*
  *Vic Duggan's Team 26*
  Vic Duggan 9, Frank Dolan 9, Cliff
    Watson 3, Jack Arnfield 2, Hugh
    Geddes 1, Lionel Levy 1, Ken Le
    Breton (res) 1
  *Bill Roger's Team 28*
  Aub Lawson 6, Bill Rogers 5, Dent
    Oliver 5, Bill Melluish 5, Eric Chitty
    4, Dick Harris 3
  *Team Reserves Match Race (1 race – 2*
  *laps)*
  v Norman Clay:
  1st Ken Le Breton, 2nd Norman Clay

*23 January – (Sydney Sports Ground)*
  *Solo Handicap – Heat 1*
  1st – Bat Byrnes
  2nd – Ken Le Breton
  3rd – Ray Duggan
  *Final*
  1st – Norman Clay
  2nd – Bat Byrnes
  3rd – Ken Le Breton
  *Junior Scratch Race Qualifier*
  1st – Keith Ryan
  2nd – Norman Clay
  3rd – Hugh Geddes
  4th – Ken Le Breton

*7 February – (Sydney Sports Ground)*
  Open Meeting – *(details unknown)*

*13 February – (Sydney Sports Ground)*
  Open Meeting – *(details unknown)*

*28 February – (Sydney Show Ground)*
  Open Meeting – *(details unknown)*

**1948/49**

*19 November – (Sydney Sports Ground)*
Four-Team Competition
*East 18* – Moff Jones 6, Frank Pritchard
6, Ted Argall 4, J. Jack Taylor 2
*North 17* – Ken Le Breton 5, Don
Lawson 5, Alec Hunter 4, A. Wall 3
*South 6* – Eddie Phelps 3, Norman Field
3, Ehret 0, Paterson 0
*West 6* – Ron Phillips 2, Doug Ible 2,
Arthur Trudgitt 1, Jock Hollis 1
*Special Handicap Event*
*Final:*
1st – Ken Le Breton
2nd – Gruff Garland
3rd – Bill Melluish
4th – Jock Hollis
5th – Keith Ryan
*26 November – (Sydney Sports Ground)*
Four-Team Competition
*North 17* – Ken Le Breton 6, Alec
Hunter 6, A. Wall 4, Clive Gressor 1
*East 13* – Moff Jones 6, Frank Pritchard
4, Ted Argall 3, ? Williams 0
*South 10* – Keith Ryan 5, Frank Malouf
2, Norman Field 2, Eddie Phelps 1
*West 7* – Doug Ible 3, Ron Phillips 2,
Arthur Trudgitt 1, Jock Hollis 0
*Scratch Race Event*
*Qualifying Heat:*
1st – Ken Le Breton
2nd – J. Jack Taylor
3rd – Keith Ryan
4th – Aub Lawson
*Final*
1st – Ken Le Breton
2nd – Bill Melluish
3rd – Eddie Phelps
4th – Gruff Garland
*3 December – (Sydney Sports Ground*
*Scratch Race Event(3 laps) Qualifier*
1st – Ken Le Breton
2nd – Gruff Garland
3rd – Bill Melluish

4th – Jack Arnfield
*Scratch Race Final:*
1st – Aub Lawson
2nd – Ken Le Breton
3rd – Jock Hollis
*Handicap Race*
1st – Bill Melluish
2nd – Jack Arnfield
3rd – Bat Byrnes
4th – Jock Hollis
5th – Ken Le Breton
6th – Aub Lawson
*Handicap Qualifier:*
1st – Bill Melluish
2nd – Ken Le Breton
3rd – Eric Chitty
*10 December – (Sydney Sports Ground)*
*Sports Ground Team 25*
Vic Duggan 9, Ray Duggan 7, Jock
Hollis 5, Ken Le Breton 2, Jack Arnfield
1, Cliff Watson 1, Moff Jones 0
*The Rest 29*
Bill Rogers 7, Aub Lawson 7, Graham
Warren 7, Bill Melluish 5, Norman
Parker 1, Eric Chitty 1, Bat Byrnes 1
*Grosskreutz Handicap Qualifier:*
1st – Don Lawson
2nd – Ken Le Breton
3rd – Norman Parker
*Grosskreutz Handicap Final:*
1st – Arthur Payne
2nd – Don Lawson
3rd – Bat Byrnes
4th – Graham Warren
5th – Ken Le Breton
6th – Bill Rogers
*17 December – (Sydney Sports Ground)*
*Best Pairs:*
Alec Statham / Eric Chitty 14
Aub Lawson / Ken Le Breton 9
Norman Parker / Bill Melluish 9
Ray Duggan / Cliff Watson 9
Graham Warren / Gruff Garland 9

Bill Rogers / Arthur Payne 4

*Parkinson Solo Handicap Qualifying Heat*:

1st – Arthur Payne

2nd– Bat Byrnes

3rd – Ken Le Breton

*18 December – (Broadmeadow, Newcastle)*

*Stars Senior Handicap Qualifier*

1st – Ken Le Breton

2nd – Don Lawson

3rd – Arthur Payne

*Stars Handicap Final*:

1st – Ken Le Breton

2nd – Frank Malouf

3rd – Don Lawson

*International Scratch Race Qualifying Heat*:

1st –Vic Duggan

2nd – Ken Le Breton

3rd – Cliff Watson

*International Scratch Race Final*: 1st –Vic Duggan

2nd – Aub Lawson

3rd – Ken Le Breton

*24 December – (Sydney Sports Ground)*

*Sydney Sports Ground 24*

Vic Duggan 9, Ken Le Breton 6, Jack Arnfield 3, Ray Duggan 3, Frank Dolan 2, Jock Hollis 1, Eric Chitty (res) (dnr)

*Newcastle (NSW) 30*

Aub Lawson 8, Norman Parker 7, Arthur Payne 4, Bill Melluish 3, Dennis Parker (res) 3, Bill Rogers 3, Cliff Watson 2

*Christmas Scratch Race (3 laps) Qualifier*

1st – Aub Lawson

2nd – Ken Le Breton

3rd – Norman Parker

*Van Praag Handicap Qualifying Heat*:

1st – Ken Le Breton

2nd – Frank Malouf

3rd – Norman Parker

*Van Praag Handicap Final*:

1st – Ken Le Breton

2nd – Frank Malouf

3rd – Dennis Parker

*27 December (Newcastle)*

*Seniors Stars Handicap Qualifying Heat*

1st – Don Lawson

2nd – Frank Pritchard

3rd – Ken Le Breton

*1 January 1949 – (Sydney Show Ground)*

*New South Wales Championship*

Bill Rogers 14, Aub Lawson 13, Graham Warren 11, Bat Byrnes 11, Ray Duggan 9, Gruff Garland 9, Bill Melluish 9, Norman Parker 8, Alec Statham 7, Vic Duggan 6, Ken Le Breton 5, Cliff Watson 4, Jack Chignell 4, Jack Arnfield 2, Jock Hollis 0, Ron Mason 0

*7 January – (Sydney Sports Ground)*

*New South Wales 73*

Aub Lawson 17, Vic Duggan 16, Cliff Watson 11, Ken Le Breton 9, Ray Duggan 7, Graham Warren 7, Bat Byrnes 6

The Rest 31

Alec Statham 8, Norman Parker 7, Eric Chitty 6, Bill Rogers 6, Arthur Atkinson 4, Moff Jones 0, Ted Argall 0

*14 January – (Sydney Sports Ground)*

*Sydney Sports Ground 33*

Vic Duggan 7, Jack Arnfield 7, Ray Duggan 7, Eric Chitty 6, Ken Le Breton 5, Moff Jones (res) 1, Frank Dolan 0

*Sydney Royale 21*

Alec Statham 8, Bat Byrnes 3, Jack Chignell 3, Ron Clarke 3, Graham Warren 3, Gruff Garland 1, Ted Argall (res) (dnr)

*Handicap Event Qualifier*

1st – Frank Malouf

2nd – Bat Byrnes

3rd – Ken Le Breton

*Scratch Race Qualifying Heat*

1st – Aub Lawson

2nd – Eric Chitty

3rd – Graham Warren

4th – Ken Le Breton

*15 January — (Sydney Show Ground)*
  *Australian Two-Lap Championship*
  Vic Duggan 14, Aub Lawson 13, Alec
    Statham 12, Ray Duggan 12, Norman
    Parker 10, Jack Biggs 9, Graham
    Warren 8, Bat Byrnes 8, Ted Argall
    (res) 5, Arthur Atkinson 5, Cliff Watson
    5, Eric Chitty 4, Jack Chignell 3, Jack
    Arnfield (res) 3, Bill Melluish 3, Bill
    Rogers 3, Ken Le Breton 3, Gruff
    Garland (res) 0, Ron Clarke 0

*21 January — (Sydney Sports Ground)*
  *International Speedway Club 32*
  Aub Lawson 9, Ray Duggan 8, Ken Le
    Breton 6, Jack Arnfield 5, Cliff Watson
    4, Lionel Levy 0
  *Norman Parker's Team 22*
  Bill Rogers 7, Arthur Atkinson 5,
    Norman Parker 4, Cliff Parkinson 4,
    Eric Chitty 1, Moff Jones (res) 1, Alec
    Statham 0
  *Senior Scratch Race Qualifier*
  1st — Bill Rogers
  2nd — Bat Byrnes
  3rd — Ken Le Breton
  4th — Arthur Atkinson

*22 January 1949 — (Sydney Show Ground)*
  *Sydney Royale 31*
  Graham Warren 8, Jack Chignell 7, Alec
    Statham 6, Bat Byrnes 5, Ernie
    Brecknell 4, Ken Blair (res) 1, Ted
    Argall 0
  *Sydney Sports Ground 23*
  Ray Duggan 9, Lionel Levy 5, Eric
    Chitty 4, Jack Chignell 2, Frank
    Malouf 2, Ken Le Breton 1, Moff
    Jones (res) (dnr)
  *Scratch Race Qualifier*

1st — Ernie Brecknell
2nd — Ken Le Breton
3rd — Ken Blair

*28 January 1949 — (Sydney Sports Ground)*
  *Champion of Champions*
  Vic Duggan 9, Ray Duggan 7, Aub
    Lawson 6, Bat Byrnes 5, Cliff Watson
    4, Graham Warren 4, Bill Rogers 3,
    Arthur Atkinson 3, Frank Malouf 3,
    Moff Jones 3, Ken Le Breton 2, Jack
    Arnfield 2, Lionel Levy (res) 2
  *Scratch Race Qualifier*
  1st — Graham Warren
  2nd — Ray Duggan
  3rd — Ken Le Breton
  4th — Aub Lawson
  *Open Handicap Qualifier*:
  1st — Ken Le Breton
  2nd — Allan Wall
  3rd — Bill Rogers
  *Open Handicap Final*
  1st — Lionel Levy
  2nd — Bat Byrnes
  3rd — Don Lawson
  4th — Ken Le Breton
  5th — Frank Malouf

*4 February — (Sydney Sports Ground)*
  *Australian 3 laps Championship*
  Aub Lawson 14, Jack Biggs 11, Graham
    Warren 10, Eric Chitty 10, Ken Le
    Breton 9, Bat Byrnes 9, Ray Duggan
    9, Vic Duggan 8, Norman Parker 8,
    Alec Statham 6, Jack Chignell 6, Jack
    Arnfield 6, Bill Longley 6, Cliff
    Watson 4, Bill Rogers 2, Gruff
    Garland 2, Frank Malouf (res) 0, Moff
    Jones (res) 0

## 1949/50

*18 November — (Sydney Sports Ground)*
  *3-Lap Solo Race*:
  1st — Ken Le Breton
  2nd — Junior Bainbridge

3rd — Alec Hunter
4th — Keith Ryan
*Handicap Final*:
1st — Ken Le Breton

2nd – Alec Hunter
3rd – Noel Watson
2-Lap Rolling Start Race
1st – Ken Le Breton
2nd – Jack Arnfield
*19 November – (Sydney Show Ground)*
Possibles 32
Jack Arnfield 9, Junior Bainbridge 8, Bill
Rogers 5, Allan Wall 4, Keith Ryan 4,
Gruff Garland 2
Probables 22
Ken Le Breton 8, Bill Melluish 6, Alec
Hunter 3, Gardiner 2, Ted Argall 2,
Lionel Levy 1
*25 November – (Sydney Sports Ground)*
Sydney Speedway Cup
Ken Le Breton 15, Jack Arnfield 14,
Norman Clay 13, Junior Bainbridge
12, Gruff Garland 10, Alec Hunter 10,
Bill Rogers 8, Keith Ryan 7, Jack
Gates 6, Ron Mason 6, Les Hewitt 6,
Ted Argall 3, Geoff Pymar 3, Allan
Wall 3, Jack Taylor 2, Lionel Levy 2,
Lionel Benson 1, Bill Melluish 0
*2 December – (Sydney Sports Ground)*
New South Wales 36
Ken Le Breton 9, Aub Lawson 8,
Norman Clay 8, Jack Arnfield 4,
Graham Warren 4, Bill Melluish 3
The Rest 17
Gordon McGregor 6, Lionel Levy 5,
Keith Ryan 4, Geoff Pymar 2, Bill
Rogers 0, Junior Bainbridge 0, Ted
Argall 0
*3 December – (Sydney Show Ground)*
New South Wales 77
Ken Le Breton 17, Aub Lawson 16,
Graham Warren 16, Norman Clay 12,
Jack Arnfield 9, Bill Melluish 5, Alec
Hunter 2, Gruff Garland (res) dnr
England 31
Bill Kitchen 11, Jack Parker 9, Ron
Clarke 4, Freddie Williams 3, Howdy
Byford 2, Cyril Roger 1, Dent
Oliver 1

*9 December – (Sydney Sports Ground)*
New South Wales Championship
Aub Lawson 15, Graham Warren 13, Bill
Longley 11, Ken Le Breton 11,
Norman Clay 11, Junior Bainbridge 9,
Jack Arnfield 8, Cyril Roger 7, Ray
Duggan 6, Ron Clarke 6, Freddie
Williams 6, Lionel Levy 5, Jack Parker
5, Bill Kitchen 5, Bill Rogers (res) 1,
Dent Oliver 1, Howdy Byford 0
*10 December – (Maribyrnong, Melbourne)*
Australian 3-Lap Championship
Bill Kitchen 14, Bill Longley 14, Jack
Biggs 13, Aub lawson 13, Norman
Lindsay 9, Ken Le Breton 9, Jack
Parker 8, Jack Young 7, H. Down (res)
7, Bill Maddern 6, Jack Bibby 6, Bob
Leverenz 6, Ron Hyde 4, R. King (res)
2, Harold Tapscott 2, W. Reynolds 0
*16 December – (Sydney Sports Ground)*
Sports Ground 26.5
Bill Kitchen 7, Ray Duggan 6, Ken le
Breton 6, Howdy Byford 3, Cyril
Roger 2, Dennis Parker (res) 1, Jack
Arnfield 1, Frank Dolan (res) 0.5
Show Ground 27.5
Jack Parker 9, Graham Warren 9,
Norman Clay 7, Freddie Williams 1.5,
Lionel Levy 1, Dent Oliver 0, Alec
Hunter (res) dnr, Ted Argall (res) dnr
Scratch Race Final
1st – Graham Warren
2nd – Ken Le Breton
3rd – Norman Clay
4th – Ray Duggan
*17 December – 1st Test (Sydney Show Ground)*
Australia 76
Jack Biggs 18, Aub Lawson 16, Graham
Warren 14, Norman Clay 13, Ken Le
Breton 10, Bill Longley 5, Jack
Arnfield (res) dnr, Alec Hunter (res)
dnr
England 32
Bill Kitchen 10, Jack Parker 9, Ron
Clarke (res) 6, Freddie Williams 5,

Cyril Roger 2, Oliver Hart 0, Dent
Oliver 0, Howdy Byford (res) 0

23 December — (Sydney Sports Ground)
Australian 2-Lap Championship
Aub Lawson 15, Graham Warren 13,
Jack Biggs 12, Freddie Williams 11, Bill
Longley 11, Ron Clarke 9, Ray
Duggan 8, Jack Parker 8, Cyril Roger
6, Ken Le Breton 5, Norman Clay 5,
Bill Kitchen 5, Oliver Hart 3, Alec
Hunter (res) 3, Junior Bainbridge 3,
Lionel Levy 2, Jack Arnfield 1

30 December — (Sydney Sports Ground)
Old Masters 28
Ron Clarke 7, Bill Longley 7, Bill
Kitchen 6, Jack Parker 5, Oliver Hart
2, Bill Rogers 1, Ray Duggan 0
New Boys 26
Graham Warren 7, Ken Le Breton 6,
Cyril Roger 4, Norman Clay 4,
Freddie Williams 3, Dent Oliver 2

6 January 1950 — 2nd Test (Sydney Sports
Ground)
Australia 67
Aub Lawson 16, Graham Warren 15,
Jack Biggs 13, Ken Le Breton 11, Bill
Longley 7, Norman Clay 4, Alec
Hunter (res) 1, Jack Arnfield (res) 0
England 41
Jack Parker 11, Oliver Hart 7, Ron
Clarke 6, Cyril Roger 6, Bill Kitchen
5, Freddie Williams 5, Howdy Byford
(res) 1, Dent Oliver (res) 0

13 January — (Sydney Sports Ground)
Sports Ground Spartans 36
Ken Le Breton 9, Jack Biggs 9, Cyril
Roger 7, Ray Duggan 6, Bill Longley
4, Howdy Byford 1
Maitland Hunters 18
Aub Lawson 7, Keith Ryan 3, Oliver
Hart 3, Junior Bainbridge 2, Ron
Clarke 2, Bill Melluish 1

14 January — (Sydney Show Ground)
Australian 4-Lap Championship
Jack Parker 15, Aub Lawson 11, Bill

Longley 10, Cyril Roger 8, Merv
Harding 8, Norman Clay 7, Jack Biggs
7, Ken Le Breton 7, Lionel Levy (res)
7, Oliver Hart 6, Les Hewitt 6, Freddie
Williams 5, Ray Duggan 5, Ron
Clarke 5, Dent Oliver 4, Alec Hunter
3, Ted Argall (res) 2, Jack Arnfield 1

20 January — (Sydney Sports Ground)
Sports Ground 26
Ken Le Breton 8, Jack Biggs 6, Bill
Longley 5, Ray Duggan 5, Arthur
Bush 2, Don Lawson 0, Frank Dolan
(res) 0
The Rest 25
Graham Warren 6, Norman Clay 5, Alec
Hunter 4, Merv Harding 4, Lionel
Levy 3, Jack Baxter 3

21 January — 3rd Test (Exhibition Oval,
Brisbane)
Australia 72
Aub Lawson 17, Graham Warren 16, Jack
Biggs 14, Keith Gurtner 9, Ken Le
Breton 8, Keith Cox 8, Dick Smythe
(res) 0, Bert Spencer (res) 0
England 35
Jack Parker 12, Oliver Hart 9, Dent
Oliver 5, Ron Clarke 3, Freddie
Williams 3, Cyril Roger 1, Howdy
Byford (res) 1, Dennis Parker (res) 1

27 January — (Sydney Sports Ground)
Scratch Race Qualifier
1st — Ken Le Breton
2nd — Frank Dolan
3rd — Arthur Bush
Scratch Race Final
1st — Ken Le Breton
2nd — Merv Harding
Triangular Inter-State Match Race
1st — Keith Gurtner
2nd — Ken Le Breton
3rd — Merv Harding

28 January — 4th Test (Sydney Show Ground)
Australia 68
Aub Lawson 18, Ken Le Breton 15,
Graham Warren 11, Bill Longley 9,

Lionel Levy (res) 7, Jack Biggs 5, Keith
Gurtner 3, Merv Harding 0
*England 40*
Oliver Hart 11, Jack Parker 11, Dent
Oliver 6, Ron Clarke 5, Cyril Roger
4, Freddie Williams 3 Dennis Parker
(res) 0, Howdy Byford (res) dnr
*2 February – (Auckland NZ)*
*British Empire Pairs*
1st – (England No.1 Team) – Norman
Parker 11 / Malcolm Craven 5 = 16
2nd – (Australia) – Ken Le Breton 9 /
Les Hewitt 5 = 14
3rd – (New Zealand No.1 Team) –
Bruce Abernethy / Dick Campbell =
13
4th – (England No.2 Team) – Ron
Mason / Gil Craven = 10
5th – (New Zealand No.2 Team) –
George Mudgway / Harold Fairhurst
= 7
*4 February – (Wellington NZ)*
*International Best Pairs (as above)*
Ken won five races and came second in
the other race – *(details unknown)*
*11 February – (Palmerston North NZ)*
*Best Pairs: Australia v Palmerston North (as
above)*
Ken won all six races – *(details unknown)*

**1950/51**

*17 November – (Sydney Sports Ground)*
*Golden Helmet Match Race (two laps –
rolling start)*
v Lionel Van Praag: Van Praag won 2–0
*25 November – (Sydney Show Ground)*
Ken reached the Scratch Race Final
(over 3 laps)
1st – Ken Le Breton
2nd – Noel Watson
3rd – Allan Quinn
4th – Arthur Payne
*1 December – (Sydney Sports Ground)*
*Scratch Race Qualifier*

*16 February – (Auckland NZ)*
*Open Individual Meeting –*
5 Handicap Races – Ken won four and
came second in the other
1 Scratch race – Ken won – *(details
unknown)*
*17 February – (Sydney Sports Ground)*
*Handicap Qualifier*
1st – Don Lawson (100yds)
2nd – Ken Le Breton (140yds)
3rd – Lionel Levy (120yds)
*Scratch Race Qualifier*
1st – Ken Le Breton
2nd – Lionel Levy
3rd – Bill Melluish
*Scratch Race Final*
1st – Keith Ryan
2nd – Lionel Levy
3rd – Ken Le Breton

*Australia won series 6 – 1. Other Series scores:*

*4 February – 5th Test (Sydney)*
Australia 68 England 40
*11 February – 6th Test (Melbourne)*
Australia 50 England 58
*17 February – 7th Test (Adelaide)*
Australia 70 England 38

1st – Ken Le Breton
2nd – Noel Watson
3rd – Arhtur Payne
*Scratch Race Final*
1st – Jack Arnfield
2nd – Ken Le Breton
3rd – Noel Watson
4th – Jack Gates
*6 December – Paramatta*
*Paramatta 30*
Noel Watson 8, Arthur Payne 7, Keith
Ryan 7, Allan Quinn 6, Allan Wall 1,
Brian Gorman 1

*Overseas 24*

Aub Lawson 9, Jack Gates 6, Ken Le Breton 4, Don Lawson 3, Huck Flynn 1, Clive Gressor 1, Frank Malouf 1

*13 December — Paramatta*

*Paramatta 26*

Ken Le Breton 6, Noel Watson 6, Dick Seers 5, Don Lawson 5, Jack Chignell 3, George Wall 1, Graham Warren 0

*Newcastle 28*

Aub Lawson 9, Keith Ryan 6, Bill Melluish 6, Allan Quinn 5, Huck Flynn 1, H. Tech 1

*16 December — 1st Test (Sydney Show Ground)*

*Australia 63*

Aub Lawson 18, Graham Warren 17, Ken Le Breton 11, Lionel Van Praag 7, Keith Ryan 6, Bill Melluish 4, Allan Quinn (res) 0, Noel Watson (res) 0

*England 45*

Jack Parker 14, Eddie Rigg 10, Eric Williams 10, Tommy Miller 5, Bob Fletcher 3, Derrick Tailby 3, Reg Fearman (res) 0, Fred Yates (res) dnr

*20 December — Paramatta*

*Paramatta 31*

Arthur Payne 7, Noel Watson 7, Dick Seers 5, Ken Le Breton 4, Jack Chignell 4, Don Lawson 4

*Bathurst 21*

Graham Warren 9, Lionel Levy 8, Alec Hunter 3, Phil Leth 1, Harold Bull 0, Bill Jamieson 0

*Scratch Race Final*

1st — Graham Warren

2nd — Aub Lawson

3rd — Doug McLachlan

4th — Ken Le Breton

*22 December — (Sydney Sports Ground)*

*New South Wales Championship*

Jack Parker 15, Aub Lawson 12, Keith Ryan 11, Eddie Rigg 10, Jack Arnfield 10, Tommy Miller 9, Ken Le Breton 8, Graham Warren 8, Dick Seers 8, Jack Gates 7, Eric Williams 6, Derrrick Tailby 5, Noel Watson 5, Bob Fletcher 3, Lionel Van Praag 2, Allan Quinn 1

*26 December — Paramatta*

*Cumberland Match Race*

v Aub Lawson:

(Lawson won — further details unknown)

*5 January 1951 — 2nd Test (Sydney Sports Ground)*

*Australia 65*

Aub Lawson 15, Jack Gates 15, Keith Ryan 13, Ken Le Breton 7, Jack Arnfield 5, Lionel Van Praag 5. Dick Seers (res) 5, Lionel Levy (res) 0

*England 42*

Jack Parker 16, Eric Williams 10, Eddie Rigg 8, Bob Fletcher 5, Tommy Miller 2, Reg Fearman (res) 1, Derrick Tailby 0, Fred Yates (res) dnr

*(This was the match that claimed Ken's life, on the last bend of the last lap of the last race.)*

Australia won series 7-0. Other results:

*27 January — 3rd Test (Sydney Show Ground)*

Australia 60 England 48

*2 February — 4th Test (Bathurst Sports Ground NSW)*

Australia 67 England 40

*7 February — 5th Test (Kilburn Adelaide)*

Australia 58.5 England 49.5

*9 February — 6th Test (Brisbane Exhibition)*

Australia 60 England 48

*10 February — 7th Test (Sydney Show Ground*

Australia 60 England 48

*Note*: The author would be grateful in receiving confirmation of any such information regarding any updates or missing particulars, which then hopefully will be included in an updated version in the future.

This then concludes the statistics section, as is known. Once again the author thanks those who generously helped in providing information for this massive task. If you feel you can add any further information etc. or wish to contact the author, please do so, c/o the publisher.

> *My heart lies in a land foreign*
> *among kindred spirits and brothers highborn*
> *we are nobody's children, are we,*
> *how could I ever abandon such as thee,*
> *their future is bright and bold,*
> *believe me, that is a story, yet to be told.*

> Ken Le Breton

# INDEX